P&O Princess

P&O Princess
The Cruise Ships

Roger Cartwright

The
HISTORY
Press

First published 2009

The History Press
The Mill, Brimscombe Port
Stroud, Gloucestershire, GL5 2QG
www.thehistorypress.co.uk

British Library Cataloguing in Publication Data.
A catalogue record for this book is available from the British Library.

ISBN 978 0 7524 4845 9

Typesetting and origination by The History Press
Printed in Great Britain

Contents

Acknowledgements

Thanks are due to P&O Cruises, Princess Cruises, Mike O'Dwyer and Clive Harvey for the use of a number of the photographs in this book. Grateful thanks are also due to Robert Lloyd for permission to use his wonderful paintings, David Dingle of Carnival plc, Felicity Wann of P&O Cruises, Pieter Van Der Schee of Princess Cruises and to my editor at the History Press, Amy Rigg, for all her advice and support. Special thanks needs to be given to my wife June and to Melanie Carter for helping maintain the flow. Every effort has been made to acknowledge ownership of photographic and authentic material. Any ommissions will be rectified in subsequent editions.

Note on the Text

GRT (Gross Registered Tonnage) is not, as many in the media make the mistake of saying, a measurement of weight. It is actually a measurement of enclosed space, i.e. volume. The volume of a merchant ship reflects its capacity and is thus of more importance than the weight to the owner. In the case of merchant ships the word tonne comes from the Anglo-Saxon *tun* meaning barrel. For medieval ship owners the number of barrels the vessel could carry was of prime importance. There are still inns and pubs in the UK named 'The Three Tuns' whose sign is three barrels.

In this text the GRT in the first part has been rounded up or down to the nearest 500 tonnes. In the list of ships it is more detailed. However, as GRT changes as ships are altered it is indicative rather than substantive. As an example, the *Normandie* of the 1930s had a GRT of 79,280 when she entered service, yet when the *Queen Mary* came out she exceeded this figure and so the French Line refitted *Normandie* with an enclosed café grill at the stern. It didn't weigh much but it was enclosed and so it increased the GRT to 82,799 compared to *Queen Mary*'s 80,774, making *Normandie* once again the world's biggest ship at the time and restoring French national pride.

Foreword

The wind in your hair; the salty smell of the sea; the glistening water, with a new skyline appearing behind it; nothing much in our modern world matches the excitement of standing at the railing of a ship on your way to another port to explore. The romance of life on board 'in the olden days' (as my children call it when I go on about the past) has left a lasting impression right through to our current time, when there is still a great deal of anticipation about holidays on the high seas.

P&O Cruises is arguably the most iconic cruise brand in the world and, together with Orient Line, was a true pioneer of the cruise industry. Many may not realise that it was its American sister, Princess Cruises, acquired by P&O in 1974, that for many years was the driver of its cruise business. The Island Princess entered homes on both sides of the Atlantic through the highly popular *Love Boat*® television series, and played a huge part in promoting a new era of cruising.

With this new era came the big ships. Grand Princess, built in 1998, was the biggest cruise ship in the world by far at that time and introduced a whole new range of on board experiences, from twenty-four-hour restaurants and flexible dining times to weddings at sea, taken by the captain, and balconies on more than half of the rooms. It helped to make cruising more popular than it had ever been (and my children are some of the greatest fans, testament I think of how cruising has changed).

This book details the first P&O and Orient liners from the end of the nineteenth century, through to the most advanced P&O Cruises and Princess superliners of the twenty-first century, with their innovative features, and ships of several related companies like P&O Cruises (Australia), British India and Swan Hellenic. Roger has a wealth of experience and, combined with his enthusiasm, has made this an enjoyable read and source of reference to all those who have cruised with these lines.

Pieter van der Schee
Head of Brand Marketing with Princess Cruises

About the Author

International author and speaker Dr Roger Cartwright was born in Manchester, England and worked as a teacher in the city before becoming a headteacher in Kent. In 1989 he switched careers and became a lecturer in management in higher education. He moved to Scotland in 1996 and retired in 2000 as the Director of the Centre for Customer Relations at Perth College – a constituent partner of the University of the Highlands and Islands.

Roger is the author of twenty-six books on management, business, customer relations and teams and leadership. His works have been published in the UK, the USA, India, Greece and China. He is also the co-author of the first comprehensive study of the cruise industry. Later, with Clive Harvey, he wrote *Cruise Britannia* about the British and cruising, published in 2004 and revised in 2008. They then wrote *The Saga Sisters*, a book dedicated to the ex-Norwegian America / Cunard liners *Vistafjord* and *Sagafjord* currently sailing as *Saga Ruby* and *Saga Rose*, a book that sold out the first edition in less than five months.

In 2002 Roger was asked for his input into a Government report about possible mergers within the UK cruise industry involving P&O Cruises and Royal Caribbean.

Roger spent a number of years as a consultant to a major air carrier and has worked in New York, Boston, Los Angeles and Atlanta helping to train airline staff. He has also worked in India.

For eighteen years Roger was attached to the Navy Days organisation at Plymouth and later Portsmouth with the rank of Lt-Cdr Royal Naval Reserve. He is currently a life trustee of the Canadian Naval Memorial to the corvette HMCS *Sackville* preserved in Halifax.

He has presented a series of maritime-themed talks on a number of cruise ships for both UK, other European, Australian, US and Canadian passengers and makes a point of matching the talks to the itinerary being followed.

Together with his wife June he lives in Crieff (Scotland) where they have a large collection of teddy bears. Roger is an avid railway modeller of both UK and US prototypes. Roger also made a brief appearance in the feature film *Rocket Post* that won the Grand Prize at the 2004 Stonybrook Film Festival in New York.

PART 1

History

At the beginning of the twenty-first century the business names that seemed to be gaining great prominence in the media were those of the companies that had done the most to pioneer new ways of bringing the world closer together. Microsoft, AOL, Dell, Cisco, Yahoo, Nokia were as well known in Glasgow, Atlanta and Kobe as they were in London and New York. The world apparently belonged to the new technologies. For much of the twentieth century, other types of companies had dominated the headlines, as groundbreaking in their time as the computer and communications companies are today. Ford, Boeing, Marconi and Edison were known the world over. So were Cunard, French Line, Italian Line, Nord Deutsche Lloyd, Hamburg Amerika, Royal Mail, Matson Line, United States Line, Canadian Pacific and Peninsular and Orient. They were the owners of the largest movable objects ever constructed – the great ocean liners. The names of their ships could be quoted by everybody, from small boys to the CEOs of major corporations: *Mauretania*, *United States*, *Ile de France*, *Bremen*, *Normandie*, *Queen Mary* and the largest passenger ship ever built until 1996, the *Queen Elizabeth*.

P&O Princess on which the sun never sets – the bow decoration on the company's vessels. (Roger Cartwright)

One of the best-known shipping industry names in the UK and the countries of the British Empire was that of the Peninsular and Oriental Steam Navigation Company – P&O. The company was less well known in the US and yet it is there that much of its recent growth has been largely achieved.

The passenger jet airliner in the 1950s was presumed to have spelt the doom of the passenger liner and indeed many older liners were scrapped and not replaced in the 1960s and '70s. However, the approximate investment in new vessels for the cruise industry between 1990 and 2008 (including vessels on order at the time of writing and due for delivery by 2008) has been well over $8,056,000,000 at 2001 prices. This figure represents just the investment in new hardware. The actual costs of the industry are much higher as it is a sector that is highly labour and oil fuel intensive.

P&O can trace its origins back to 1834 and there seems no reason, given the position of P&O Princess in the cruise market, why its house flag should not be flying over cruise ships in 2034 – no small achievement for a company that appeared to be in a dead industry in the 1960s. The company's US operation, Princess Cruises, whose vessels appeared in the best-selling television series *The Love Boat* and whose slogan became 'It's more than a cruise, it's the Love Boat®', was one of the major vehicles used by P&O to gain US market share and provided a major introduction to cruising for many in North America and later in the UK through their television screens.

THE EARLY YEARS

In 1834 Shetland-born Arthur Anderson and Ostend-born Brodie McGhie Wilcox from Newcastle-upon-Tyne, acting as ship brokers, advertised a paddle steamer sailing from London to Lisbon, the capital of Portugal and situated on the Iberian Peninsular. The vessel used was the *Royal Tar* owned and captained by Captain Richard Bourne and his Dublin and London Steam Packet Company. The attempt to raise the capital for Anderson and Wilcox's own company, the name of which was to be the Peninsular Steam Navigation Company, was unsuccessful and the pair continued to act purely as ship brokers. However, the partners had assisted both the Spanish and Portuguese royal families by delivering supplies (and British troops) when both thrones were under threat of civil war in 1834 and 1835 and they received royal assistance and favour so that they were able to set up their company in 1835. The red and yellow of Spain and the blue and white of Portugal were incorporated into their diagonally quartered house flag – a house flag that is still used today.

By 1837 the company was operating six chartered steamers and had built four new ships of its own. One of the chartered steamers, the *William Fawcett*, was used on a Lisbon-Madeira service. It is this vessel that was the first 'regular' P&O ship, as the *Royal Tar* was initially chartered for just one voyage.

In 1837 the company was awarded the lucrative Admiralty mail contract worth over £29,000 (a considerable sum in the 1830s) to carry the mails between London, Spain, Portugal and on to Gibraltar on a weekly basis. In addition the company was to provide a feeder service along the Spanish coast from Malaga to Gibraltar and from Lisbon to Madeira in addition to a service between Liverpool and Gibraltar.

The company nearly lost Arthur Anderson and his wife in September 1837 when the *Don Juan* went aground off Tarifa whilst returning from Gibraltar. Although fortunately no lives were lost, it proved impossible to salvage the vessel.

Notwithstanding the loss of the *Don Juan*, the company gained a reputation for reliability, punctuality and safety and was in profit. The Lord Governor of India, Lord Bentinck, approached the company with a view to extending the Gibraltar service as far as Alexandria in Egypt and to set up a service from Suez to India with a land journey from Alexandria to the Gulf of Suez. There was already a British Government service that linked Marseilles with Malta and then from Malta to Suez with

William Fawcett, the first P&O ship. (P&O)

the London-Marseilles portion involving a long land journey after a cross-channel ferry trip. The company showed no interest as it was not in its interest to compete directly with the Government as it might put the mail contracts in jeopardy. The next year (1840) however, the British Government itself realised that the Marseilles service was not the most practical and asked the company to extend the Iberian service to Alexandria and thence overland to Suez and on to India. The company agreed and this led to a change of title from the Peninsular Steam Navigation Company to the Peninsular and Oriental Steam Navigation Company – P&O. To operate the new service bigger vessels were required. Fortunately the *Great Liverpool* (1,312 GRT) and the *Oriental* (1,787 GRT) were available, having been built for the Transatlantic Steam Ship Company as the *Liverpool* (1838) and the *United States* (1840) respectively. The Transatlantic Steamship Company had lost out to Cunard in the bid for the North American Mails contract and thus the vessels were available for charter and, in the case of *Oriental*, purchase by P&O.

The land journey from Alexandria to Suez took thirty-six hours using a mixture of barges, river steamer and camels and the company set up a series of refreshment stops although the journey remained long and tiresome due to the heat.

By 1844 P&O had been awarded the Ceylon-Singapore-Hong Kong service and by 3 August 1853 P&O ships had reached Australia when the new steamship *Chusan* arrived in Sydney. The company also began to offer a service to China and by 1859 had reached Japan.

P&O was not without rivals. In 1856 the Calcutta & Burmah (sic) Steam Navigation Company was formed and in 1862 this became the British India Steam Company, later British India Steam Navigation (BI). In 1878 the Orient Steam Navigation Company was formed to operate to Australia via Cape Town rather than subject passengers to the heat and dust of the P&O overland route from Alexandria to Suez. British India was a major operator of troopships, a role continued until after the Second World War. In May 1914 British India and P&O amalgamated although the individual identities of the companies were retained until 1986 when the last BI ship, *Uganda*, went to the breakers. With its huge network of routes in India, the Persian Gulf and East Africa, British India had at one time the largest number of vessels sailing under the Red Ensign. Orient Line and P&O had been cooperating since the award of a joint UK-Australia contract in 1888. In 1919 P&O acquired a 51 per cent holding in Orient Line although separate identities and liveries were retained until May 1960 when P&O-Orient Lines was formed from the formal amalgamation of the two fleets.

The opening of the Suez Canal in 1869 meant the end of the trek across the desert and made the journey much more pleasant, especially as it removed the need to change ships during the journey to the East.

CRUISING

The voyages out to the East were made for necessity not pleasure. The idea of taking an ocean voyage for pleasure was a concept that had not yet arrived. An ocean voyage was still an adventure. By the 1890s it was less dangerous than in the days of sail but still not something to be undertaken lightly. Indeed the whole idea of holidays was something new. It was the railways that allowed ordinary people to take a break away from home but foreign travel was still the preserve of the well-off.

The first ocean 'pleasure' cruise was as early as 1881, when the Oceanic Yachting Company / Polytechnic Touring Association bought P&O's *Ceylon* and refitted her as a full-time cruise ship for the European market. *Ceylon* had been built in 1858 and was by 1881 surplus to P&O requirements. She proved a success for her new owners and although she changed hands a number of times was not broken up until 1907.

P&O began cruising in its own right on a regular basis in 1904 when the *Rome* of 1881 was taken out of service and converted to a full-time cruise ship named *Vectis*. She lasted in this role until 1912.

Orion in a classic Orient line location – the Suez Canal. (P&O)

Her role was then taken over by the 1909-built *Mantua*. She operated as a cruise ship between 1913 and 1914, actually being recalled from a cruise in the Baltic on 2 August 1914 for service as an AMC (Armed Merchant Cruiser) and later as a troopship. She survived the war and joined the service to Australia.

Orient Line was an even earlier entrant into the cruise business. Their *Lusitania* of 1878 (not to be confused with the famous Cunard liner of the same name) began cruising in 1887 and this move was followed by a number of the company's vessels when not employed on regular line voyages.

Cruising provided an opportunity to generate extra business during slack periods. In the main the ships used were normal liners and lacked swimming pools and many of the amenities we now associate with the cruise industry. Entertainment was minimal and it was the destinations that were being sold. The Norwegian fjords, Madeira, the Canary Islands and the Western Mediterranean were the main cruising areas for the early cruise companies – areas that are still popular cruising destinations today. A thirteen-night cruise on Orient Lines' *Ophir* in 1907 cost 13 guineas – quite a considerable sum in those days. As more and more interest was shown in cruising, a number of older ships were switched to cruising full time.

The first P&O cruise ship, the liner *Rome* of 1881, renamed *Vectis* in 1904 when she was dedicated to cruising. (P&O)

The First World War put an end to the early interest in cruising. At the end of the war, P&O, British India and Orient Lines had lost a large number of vessels to enemy action (Orient Line was to lose half of its fleet in both world wars) and rebuilding of the fleets commenced. Between the wars more and more of both the P&O and Orient Line fleets began cruising. The Orient Line ships *Orama*, *Orford*, *Oronsay*, *Otranto* and *Orontes* built in the 1920s were all converted from three-class ships to two classes (first and tourist) to make them more acceptable to cruise passengers. In 1933 the *Ormonde* of 1917 was converted to a one-class ship and spent much of her year cruising. Both revolutionary, the *Orion* of 1934 and her sister the *Orontes* of 1937 were designed both for line voyages to Australia and for cruising. Sadly the Second World War put an end to *Orontes'* career as she was sunk in 1942. Interestingly *Orontes* had an almost identical hull form to the *Strathallan* (see later) and both were to be sunk by submarines within weeks of each other during the Second World War. They had been built in the same Vickers yard at Barrow-in-Furness within two years of each other.

By 1920 P&O had also acquired the Union Steamship of New Zealand and the New Zealand Steamship companies although these acquisitions did not impact on the cruise operations. In a similar fashion to the Orient Line ships of that era, two of the M Class ships of P&O dating from the early

Below left: Deck quoits Edwardian style. (Source unknown)

Below right: Deck quoits twenty-first-century style. (Roger Cartwright)

1920s, *Moldavia* and *Mongolia*, were altered in 1931 to become one-class ships for cruising. The four R Class ships, *Rajputana*, *Ranchi*, *Ranpurna* and *Rawalpindi* (famous for her heroic action against the *Sharnhorst* and the *Gneisenau* in 1939), were sent cruising in the Mediterranean when not engaged in the UK-Bombay service. The beautiful *Viceroy of India* of 1928 was a regular cruise ship out of Southampton.

In 1931 P&O introduced the *Strathnaver*, followed by her sister *Strathaird* in 1932. With three funnels (two of them dummies) and a first for P&O, a white hull, these vessels became known as the 'White Sisters'. With their white hulls and yellow funnels they introduced the livery that is still seen today. Orient Line ships had a similar funnel but a corn-coloured hull. Three more 'Strath' boats followed before the war, *Strathmore*, *Strathallan* and *Stratheden*, but with only one funnel. *Strathallan* of 1938 only undertook a few cruises before she was requisitioned for war service and sunk during the North African landings in December 1942. These ships made excellent cruise vessels and were very modern for their time.

British India had its trooping duties and regular line service to India and services around the Persian Gulf and the Indian Ocean. In 1932 the company introduced a new venture – an educational cruise for school pupils on the 1912-built troopship *Neuralia*. These cruises, mainly to Norway and the Baltic, were operated when the ship was not trooping and ran until 1935. The first was for Scottish pupils and ran from Leith to Scandinavia, with the ship chartered to the Scottish Schools Travel Trust on 25 July 1935. Her sister *Nevasa* also entered the educational cruise market between 1935 and 1937 under the auspices of the School Journeys Association of London. These educational cruises were to become an important part of the company's business post-Second World War.

Advertisement for the *Viceroy of India*'s 1935 cruising season. (P&O)

One of the White Sisters of the 1930s entices potential cruise passengers to exotic locations. (P&O)

As in the earlier conflict the P&O companies lost many vessels. The war also produced technological advances in aircraft technologies. Whilst the ocean liner still reigned supreme it was not long until the introduction of aircraft capable of crossing the Atlantic non-stop began to make inroads into the companies operating the Europe-North America liner services. The way out East seemed secure for the shipping companies and much new tonnage entered the fleet. However, swimming pools and more extensive entertainment were now required for both line voyages and cruising. The new vessels that P&O and Orient Line introduced on their services were going to have to undertake more and more extensive cruising. Between 1948 and 1954 Orient Line introduced the *Orcades*, *Oronsay* and *Orsova* (all built at the Vickers yard in Barrow), whilst P&O brought out the *Arcadia*, *Iberia*, *Himalaya* and *Chusan*. *Iberia* proved unsuited to cruising but the other ships spent more and more time on cruise operations. There was a good market for line voyages due to the assisted-passage scheme to take Britons to Australia, but this would not last forever. Modernisation occurred with *Orcades* being the first Orient Line ship to acquire air-conditioning in 1959 (a pre-requisite for a modern cruise ship) with her sisters receiving it as well over the next couple of years. *Arcadia* was modernised in order to appeal to the West Coast of the USA market (she was based in San Francisco and was a regular visitor to Alaska) whilst *Chusan* inaugurated the first of the P&O 'World Cruises' in 1959.

The earliest jet airlines could not make the Europe-Far East journey without refuelling stops and fares were expensive. There still seemed a considerable market for passenger liners out to the Far East and Australasia. Shaw Savill and Albion built the one-class *Southern Cross* and *Northern Star* for these routes and whilst P&O, Orient Line and British India rationalised their fleets there was still optimism that despite air travel, a gradual British withdrawal of troops east of Suez and the telephone (for business), a market for the liners for long journeys remained. All three companies also operated freight ships (P&O and British India in particular) and these seemed to have a promising future although their operations are beyond the scope of this book.

In 1960 the last and largest Orient Liner, *Oriana*, entered service on the Australia run. 1960 was also the year in which P&O and Orient Line became one as P&O Orient Lines following the purchase of the remaining Orient Line shares by P&O. Built by Vickers at Barrow, *Oriana* was much larger at 40,000 GRT than her 28,000 GRT predecessors. Ordered by Orient Line, she was followed in 1961 by the ship that was to become the quintessential British cruise ship – P&O's *Canberra*.

A family group on *Strathnaver* in the 1930s. (Photograph provided by the P&O 'Posh' Club)

THE *CANBERRA* ERA

Both *Canberra* and *Oriana* were the largest ships ever employed on the Far East and Australasia service. At 46,000 GRT *Canberra* was by far the largest P&O liner ever built to that date and a fitting flagship. *Canberra* served in all three traditional P&O passenger liner roles: the line service, as a cruise ship and as a troopship in the Falklands conflict of 1982. She also spanned the years between P&O's passenger operations, being a liner service with some cruises to being a purely cruise operation. Together with the *QE2* she became the best-known cruise ship within the British market.

Oriana (with her corn-coloured hull repainted white) also cruised for the company and in 1974 was switched to full-time cruising out of Australia. The mainstay of the Australian cruising market at the time was the *Fairstar* of Sitmar Line. She had been built as the *Oxfordshire* for the Bibby Line trooping service and had then served Fairstar shipping as an emigrant ship. By 1981 *Oriana* was cruising full time out of Sydney, a role she continued until withdrawn in 1986.

Canberra had an eventful career. In 1963 inbound from Australia through the Suez Canal she caught fire off Italy whilst carrying 2,238 passengers but survived. In June 1967 she nearly became trapped in the Suez Canal when Egypt and Israel went to war. She was approaching Port Said when her captain made the decision to turn around. She might have been trapped for years – some ships were not released until 1971.

Canberra became a full-time cruise ship in 1974 with the ending of the Australia service; the Boeing 747 had finally sounded the death knell for the classic ocean liner.

Canberra – the quintessential British cruise ship. (Clive Harvey)

Built as a two-class ship, it was fortunately easy to convert *Canberra* for one-class cruising. *Orsova* had been retained as her running mate during the late 1960s although she remained a two-class ship. In 1974 she went to the breakers and there were just *Canberra*, *Oriana*, *Arcadia* plus British India's *Uganda* and *Nevasa* left when *Oronsay* went to the breakers in 1975.

EDUCATIONAL CRUISING RESUMED

Educational cruises had proved successful for British India in the 1930s. The 1950s saw BI's services decimated by air transport and the decision of the UK Government to withdraw from many of its colonies and military bases east of Suez. One by one the liners and troopships were sold or scrapped. *Dunera* was a troopship built in 1937, saved and converted to an educational cruise ship in 1961. In addition to her 834 students she also provided excellent cabin class accommodation (well separated from the children) for 194 cruise passengers. A swimming pool was installed, BI livery rather than troopship livery applied, and her masts shortened so that she could transit through the Kiel Canal for Baltic cruising. She retained this role until withdrawn and scrapped in 1967. *Devonia* of 1939 was laid down as the troopship *Devonshire* for Bibby Line and was a near sister to *Dunera*. She was also converted to an educational cruise vessel in 1962 and like *Dunera* served until 1967. Their replacement was the *Uganda* of 1952. Built together with her sister *Kenya* for the UK-Cape Town-East Africa service, she served on this service until 1967. The closure of the Suez Canal due to the Six- Day War (see *Canberra* above) led to the service being closed as the ships had returned from East Africa to the UK via the Suez Canal and *Kenya* was scrapped in 1969.

Uganda was refitted in Hamburg as an educational cruise ship in 1967. The ship was extensively altered. Extra lifeboats were installed forward and cargo-handling equipment removed. Her stern area was plated in to form a lounge and two swimming pools installed, one for her 304 cabin class cruise passengers forward and another aft for her 920 students. Air conditioning was also installed. For long periods she was based in the Mediterranean with passengers and students being flown out to her. She was a very popular ship, her most successful year being 1978.

When the Argentine forces invaded the Falkland Islands on 2 April 1982 she was at Alexandria. Her passengers were disembarked at Naples and she proceeded to Gibraltar for conversion to a hospital ship. She served with great distinction, saving many British and Argentine lives.

Returned to cruising in September 1982, her cruise ship role did not last long. She was chartered to the Ministry of Defence as a troopship between 1983 and 1985. Laid up, she sailed to Kaohsiung for breaking under the name *Triton* but was blown from her berth at the breakers by Cyclone 'Wayne' and turned on her side. There is a wonderful, evocative painting by Stuart Beck of her final voyage. With her passed the idea of educational cruising, although it has recently been taken up again by the UK-based Voyages of Discovery, now part of the All Leisure Group.

BI's final passenger vessel was the *Nevasa* of 1956. A 20,500 GRT troopship, she was made redundant in that role when troop transport was switched to airliners in 1962. In 1964 she was refitted and reliveried into classic BI livery as a very modern educational cruise ship. With 308 cabin class passengers in excellent accommodation and 1,120 students, she made her first cruise for students from Staffordshire Education Authority in October 1964. Her major problem was the thirst of her engines in a period of rising oil prices. Proving uneconomic, she was withdrawn and scrapped in January 1975 after a relatively short life for such a fine ship.

The British India educational cruise ship *Uganda*. (Clive Harvey)

THE FLEET DECLINES

Oil prices and dock strikes in the UK hit the passenger shipping industry badly, with a number of fine ships going for scrap or being sold to new owners in the early 1970s. P&O Orient Lines and BI lost the 'Straths' in the 1960s and by 1979 *Orcades*, *Oronsay*, *Orsova*, *Arcadia* (cruising out of Australia from 1975–79), *Chusan*, *Himalaya* and *Iberia* had gone as had the *Reina del Mar* and a number of other Union Castle

Spirit of London, later *Sun Princess.* (P&O)

vessels, Shaw Savill's *Northern Star* and *Southern Cross* (although *Southern Cross* continued in the cruise market for a succession of owners until 2003) and Royal Mail's *Andes.* Many other fine passenger vessels from the maritime nations of the world succumbed at this time, some sold to new cruise companies but many scrapped.

Canberra herself had a narrow squeak. In June 1973 it was announced that *Canberra* would be withdrawn as uneconomic and that the cruise operations would be undertaken by *Oriana, Orsova* and the new, purpose-built *Spirit of London. Canberra* had been tried in the US cruise market but had not been a success and the newly restructured P&O was looking to make savings. Fortunately she was reprieved and converted to a one-class cruise ship and *Orsova* was withdrawn instead.

The Italian-built *Spirit of London* was P&O's first purpose-built cruise ship. A small vessel, she was purchased from her original Norwegian owners whilst building. P&O introduced her to the US market for West Coast cruises in November 1971. Following the acquisition of Princess Cruises she was transferred to the new company as the *Sun Princess.* In 1988 she was sold to Premier Cruise Lines as the *Majestic,* later renamed *Starship Majestic.* In 1997 she became the *Flamenco* of Festival Cruises and when that company failed in 2004 she was laid up before becoming the *New Flamenco* of Travelplan Cruises, a Spanish operator.

It was the nadir of the passenger shipping industry; the mighty P&O was by 1973 down to three vessels, one in the US, one in the UK and one in Australia.

PRINCESS CRUISES AND THE LOVE BOAT®

Stanley B. McDonald had founded Princess Cruises on the Western seaboard of the USA in 1965, initially using chartered vessels. His first vessel was the Canadian Pacific coastal steamer *Princess Patricia.* The anecdotal story is that the Princess brand name for the operation was chosen to fit in with the name of the vessel! The newly built *Italia* was then chartered as the *Princess Italia* followed by the charter of Costa's *Carla C* as the *Princess Carla.* Following the failure of both *Canberra* and *Spirit of London* in the US, P&O was still keen to enter such a lucrative market. Princess Cruises was purchased by P&O in 1974, although the US operation continued to operate under the Princess brand. This provided P&O with an easy entry into the US market where the P&O brand was less well known, indeed the P&O acquisition of Princess and later Sitmar Cruises is often quoted as a textbook example of how an organisation can expand into a new market by acquisition, thus retaining the customer base of the acquired company.

During 1972 Princess chartered both the *Pacific Princess* and *Island Princess* (the latter ship coming into the UK market in 2002 as the *Discovery* of the Voyages of Discovery Company) from the defunct Flagship Cruises, who had ordered the vessels in 1970. They were used to provide Princess Cruises with vessels to replace those that had been chartered to start the company. In 1977 in a marketing coup both ships were made available to Aaron Spelling Productions and became the stars of The Love Boat®, a highly successful television series starring Gavin Macleod as Captain Stubbings. Initially Princess were lukewarm about this initiative from the television production company, but soon realised the potential marketing boost it was giving them. So successful was *The Love Boat®* that even in the 1990s Princess were still using, 'It's more than a cruise, it's the Love Boat®' as a catchphrase. A revamped *Love Boat®* series was made for showing in the early years of the twenty-first century using one of the newer Princess ships.

Pacific Princess, one of the original love boats, together with the author's other love, his wife June. (Roger Cartwright)

Americans became entranced with the fun, sun and romance depicted in the series and it was just as successful when shown to UK audiences. German audiences had their own long-running show *Traumshiffe* (Dreamship) which started in the 1980s and featured the 9,570 GRT *MV Berlin* (now Saga's *Spirit of Adventure*) of Deilmann Reederie.

The appearance of a regular cruise-related soap opera on both US and UK television screens did a great deal to raise awareness of cruising as a fun experience and one for everyone and not just a wealthy minority.

In time Princess Cruises was to become one of the major US cruise lines and its growth is chronicled later in this chapter.

By the mid-1980s, P&O and Princess Cruises had the *Canberra* in the UK market, and a second vessel, *Sea Princess*, operating alongside *Oriana* out of Sydney and *Sun Princess*, *Pacific Princess* and *Island Princess* in the US. *Pacific Princess* was one of the ships that pioneered cruising up and down the Amazon – a new destination in the early 1990s but one that is commonplace today, as shown by the large new terminal at Manaus.

Built as the *Kungsholm* for by Swedish-America on both transatlantic voyages and cruises, the ship was sold to Flagship Cruises in 1975 and operated out of New York. She was acquired by the Princess Cruises operation of P&O and renamed *Sea Princess*. An extensive refit saw the removal of her forward funnel and the remodelling of the aft one, plus extensive alterations to her fittings – to the detriment of her appearance according to many purists. Initially she replaced *Arcadia* cruising out of Sydney.

Top: Amazon ferries seen from *Pacific Princess* in 1993. (Roger Cartwright)

Bottom: Pacific Princess was a pioneer of Amazon cruising in the early 1990s. To go ashore along the river the crew erected temporary landings. Here the local children enjoy a balloon from a passenger. (Roger Cartwright)

Right: Who wouldn't want to run away to sea? The officer is Roy Cookman. (P&O)

RUN AWAY TO SEA
BY
P&O-ORIENT
LINES

Europe · Australia · New Zealand · Far East · Pacific · U.S.A · Canada

In 1982 she was transferred to the UK P&O fleet as the running mate to *Canberra*. In 1995 she was given an 'ia' ending name to fit in with the naming of the ships of the UK P&O Cruises fleet. As *Victoria* she operated alongside the new *Oriana* and *Aurora* until her sale into the German cruise market in 2002 as the *Mona Lisa*. She later became *The Scholarship*, operating as a floating university.

SWAN HELLENIC

In 1930 W.F. Swan, the owner of the Swan Travel Bureau, set up a new company, Swan Hellenic, to provide cultural cruises around Greece and its islands.

In 1954 the company began to offer cruises under its own name. The first ship chartered was the *Miaoulis* and over the years a number of vessels were used, including the Turkish *Ankara*. For a number of years between 1974 and 1995 the company chartered the *Orpheus* from Epirotiki Lines before being replaced by the 12,000 GRT *Minerva*, the hull of which had been laid down as a Russian survey (spy?) ship. Swan Hellenic was acquired by P&O in 1983 but operated as a distinct brand. For the 2003 season the company ended the charter of *Minerva* and acquired the use of *Minerva 2* (one of the eight vessels made available due to the failure of Renaissance Cruises – P&O Princess eventually acquiring three of the 'R' ships), a much larger ship, reflecting the growth in this type of cruising.

Swan Hellenic cruises were for those interested in the culture of the areas they were visiting – areas that span a much greater part of the globe than the Hellenic world – the original destination for the company. Swan Hellenic did not have casinos but the cruises were accompanied by leading authorities – archaeologists, historians, art critics, politicians, statesmen, keen women and religious figures, including archbishops. A large number of shore excursions led by acknowledged experts were included in the price of the cruise. A Swan Hellenic cruise has been described as 'cruising country house style'. Sadly Carnival Group to which P&O Princess now belongs decided that the Swan Hellenic cruise brand would cease to operate from 2007 with the *Minerva 2* going to Princess Cruises as the new *Royal Princess*. However, Lord Sterling purchased the Swan Hellenic brand and the original *Minerva* (using her original name) was chartered from Voyages of Discovery (who had named her *Explorer 2*) with the product set to launch in the spring of 2008 although problems with the ship caused a delay.

A FALKLAND INTERLUDE

One of *Canberra*'s greatest moments was as the main troopship for the Falkland Islands campaign in 1982. When the Argentine invasion occurred *Canberra* was on the homeward leg of a cruise. Naval officers boarded her in secret at Gibraltar and began taking measurements. By the time she arrived in

Southampton on 5 April a helicopter deck was ready for fitting. As the troopship for 3 Commando Brigade comprising elements from the Royal Marines and the Parachute Regiment, she sailed for the Falklands. Whilst QE2 was also taken up from trade she only went as far as South Georgia. *Canberra*, 'The Great White Whale', still in her P&O livery, entered San Carlos Water on 21 May and survived the attention of the Argentine Air Force. Still with many of her regular crew on board she made a triumphant return to the UK, entering Southampton to cheering crowds on 11 July.

As discussed earlier, *Uganda* also served in the Falkland conflict and whilst her role was less glamorous and received scant public attention, it was nevertheless a vital one.

THE FLEET EXPANDS

The next Princess Cruises vessel was the strikingly modern 44,500 GRT *Royal Princess* of 1984 built in the Wartsila yard in Finland. Named by Princess Diana, she had a long career with Princess before being transferred to the P&O UK operation in 2005 as the adult-only *Artemis*. *Oriana* was withdrawn in 1988 to become a floating exhibition centre in Japan and then a floating hotel and tourist centre in China. Sadly she broke free from her moorings in a typhoon in late 2004 and was sold to Indian breakers in 2005.

For the next few years the growth was concentrated on the Princess operation. In 1988 P&O acquired the cruise operations of Sitmar Line with tonnage operating mainly in Australia and the USA. The acquired ships were the *Fairstar* in Australia with the *Fairsea*, *Fairwind* (ex-*Carinthia* and *Sylvania* of Cunard respectively) and the *Fairsky*, Sitmar's first ever new build in the US market. *Fairstar* had a very loyal Australian following and her name was kept but the other vessels were renamed *Fair Princess*, *Dawn Princess* and *Sky Princess* and integrated fully into the Princess Fleet.

1988 was the year in which the UK cruise operation was rebranded as P&O Cruises. Of great importance were the three Sitmar vessels that were building at the time of the acquisition. The 66,000 GRT *Star Princess* was originally to be named *Sitmar Fairmajesty*). After transfer to the UK in 1997 as *Arcadia* she is now *Ocean Village* and still in the fleet. Although ordered by Sitmar, the 70,000 GRT *Crown Princess* and *Regal Princess* became the biggest passenger ships not only for P&O but were only exceeded by the *Queen Mary* and the *Queen Elizabeth* in the UK passenger fleet historic lists. The acquisition of Sitmar greatly increased the Princess operation.

Fairstar was later sold back to V Ships (the owners of Sitmar) in 1993 and continued cruising out of Australia until scrapped in 1997. V Ships also re-acquired *Dawn Princess* (ex-*Fairwind*) in 1993. She was chartered to German interests and renamed *Albatros* (sic) and was broken up in 2005.

On 1 November 1983 Jeffrey Sterling (later Lord Sterling) had been appointed Chairman of the P&O Group to succeed Lord Inchcape. He successfully defended a takeover attempt by Trafalgar House (the then owners of Cunard). In 1991 P&O actually acquired part of the Cunard freighter operation when the Group purchased the container interests of Cunard-Ellerman from Trafalgar House.

Also in 1991 the *Pacific Princess*, *Island Princess* and *Canberra* were sold to the Abbey National Building Society and leased back whilst *Royal Princess* was sold to Howell Shipping and also leased back, thus providing cash for expansion.

The P&O Group celebrated its 150th anniversary in 1987. HM Queen Elizabeth II was entertained at a dinner held on board *Pacific Princess* anchored off Greenwich on 7 July.

Sea Princess spent 1979–1982 in the Australian market and was then transferred to the UK to operate out of Southampton until 1986 when she rejoined the Princess fleet, although she was to return to the UK as *Victoria* in 1995. That left only *Canberra* to service P&O's UK market. *Sun Princess* was sold in 1989 and sails on today as the *New Flamenco*.

A NEW *ORIANA*

By 1988 P&O Princess had begun to consider the replacement of *Canberra*. The UK cruise market was beginning to grow again. To be economic the new ship would need to capture at least 10 per cent of the UK market. *Canberra* had a very loyal following and the new ship would need to retain these customers. The contract for the new vessel was signed in December 1991 with Myer Weft in Papenburg, Germany. No British yard was prepared, sadly, to bid for the £200 million contract.

Named *Oriana* by HM Queen Elizabeth II, the 69,000 GRT ship entered the UK market in the spring of 1995; she was the first ever purpose-built cruise ship designed purely for the UK market. Internally and externally there were touches of *Canberra* to make the *Canberra* loyalists feel at home. A supremely elegant vessel, she quickly became very popular. She provided the UK market with up-to-date facilities including a West End-style theatre and wonderful British and Commonwealth artworks.

Canberra continued to operate alongside *Victoria* (ex-*Sea Princess*) and *Oriana* in the UK market until her withdrawal in 1997. Demand for her final cruise in September of that year far exceeded the available berths and she returned from it to a flotilla of small boats and flag-waving crowds flying her paying-off pennant. She had served the company well for thirty-six years as a liner, a cruise ship and even a troopship. Rumours that she would be sold for further service were unfounded and on 10 October 1997 she sailed for the Gadani Beach in Pakistan where she was run ashore at full speed and broken up. There were crowds at Southampton to watch her leave for the last time and the event (and their tears) made the national television news.

Initially *Canberra* was replaced by *Star Princess*, renamed *Arcadia* in 1997 for the UK market. A contract was also placed with Meyer Weft for an enlarged *Oriana* to be named *Aurora* after the Goddess of the Dawn.

Top left: Laying the keel for Britain's first purpose-built cruise ship – *Oriana*. (P&O)

Top right: Oriana, Britain's first purpose-built cruise ship, takes shape in Germany. (P&O)

Left: Air conditioned and West End style – *Oriana*'s theatre. (P&O)

Slightly larger than *Oriana* but designed to the same philosophy of a quintessentially British ship, *Aurora* made her debut in May 2000. Only a few hours into her maiden cruise a bearing went and the ship had to return to Southampton and the cruise was cancelled. It is a measure of the way P&O handled the situation by keeping passengers informed and offering full refunds and a future cruise that the mishap was turned from a potential public relations disaster into a triumph. Named by Princess Anne, the bottle did not break, leading some to say that this was an omen.

On 9 September 2001 *Aurora* made her maiden entry into New York where she disembarked cruise passengers from the UK, some of whom flew straight home whilst others undertook six-day excursions before re-joining the ship together with passengers who had flown out for the homeward leg. On 11 September the ship was at sea with the first of her short US charters. Following the terrorist attacks on New York and Washington she was routed into Boston to await her passengers, returning home via an unscheduled stop in Halifax (Nova Scotia) to pick up passengers who had been stranded in Canada and also to embark entertainers and staff including two chaplains from the UK.

John Clinch's magnificent resin figures outside *Oriana*'s cinema. (P&O)

Aurora was at the centre of a series of diplomatic rows in 2004. A number of passengers were taken ill with the Novovirus that has affected a number of cruise ships. Perfectly healthy passengers were denied entry into Greece and the Spanish Government shut the border with Gibraltar when the ship docked there. The Spanish action appears to have been more political than anything else given the long-running dispute over the sovereignty of Gibraltar.

Aurora has proved to be a very successful ship that is both modern and traditional. Her success was somewhat muted by events in January 2005 when her world cruise was delayed by days due to an engine problem. The passengers were accommodated on board and entertainment by top artists provided. Repairs in Southampton proved impossible and the cruise was cancelled at an estimated cost of £26 million.

Right: Aurora has a superb berth in Venice, only yards from St Mark's Square. (Roger Cartwright)

Below: Oceana in tropical surroundings. (Roger Cartwright)

Opposite:
Top left: The magnificent ceiling in *Oceana's* atrium. (Roger Cartwright)

Top right: Shopping mall at sea – *Oceana's* Bond Street. (Roger Cartwright)

Bottom left: Oceana and *Coral Princess* side by side in the Caribbean viewed through dockyard pipes. (Roger Cartwright)

Bottom right: No lack of sun-loungers on board *Oceana*. (Roger Cartwright)

Opposite:

Top left: A study in curves – the atrium of the *Diamond Princess.* (Roger Cartwright)

Top right: Large ship elegance – the writing room of the *Diamond Princess.* (Roger Cartwright)

Bottom left: The sitting room of the owner's suite on *Diamond Princess.* (Roger Cartwright)

Bottom right: The bedroom of the owner's suite on *Diamond Princess* with ever-smiling steward. (Roger Cartwright)

To further boost the UK fleet two of the *Dawn Princess* class (see later) were transferred to Southampton in 2003. *Ocean Princess* became and still is *Oceana* whilst *Sea Princess* became *Adonia* (as an adult-only ship). They were marketed as the new White Sisters. *Adonia* later returned to the Princess fleet reverting to her original name.

DEMERGER

On 23 October 2000 P&O Princess demerged from the main P&O Group to become a separate entity although still owned by P&O. It was this demerger that was to lay the groundwork for the later proposed merger with Royal Caribbean and the eventual absorption of P&O Princess into the Carnival Group in 2003.

PRINCESS AND THE MEGA SHIPS

The *Carnival Destiny* in 1996 was the first vessel of over 100,000 GRT. Too broad for the Panama Canal, she was to be the first of a series of Carnival 'mega' ships. Princess followed suit in 1998 with the 109,000 GRT *Grand Princess* from the Fincantieri yard. Princess developed a twin-track approach. A series of 100,000 GRT-plus mega ships were built: *Golden Princess* (2001), *Star Princess* (2002), *Caribbean Princess, Diamond Princess, Sapphire Princess* (2004), *Crown Princess* (2006) and *Emerald Princess* (2007) plus a series of slightly smaller ships ranging from 77,000-92,000 GRT: *Sun Princess* (1995), *Dawn Princess* (1997), *Sea Princess* (1998), *Ocean Princess* (2000), *Coral Princess* (2002) and *Island Princess* (2003).

Diamond Princess had been laid down as *Sapphire Princess* with the original *Diamond Princess* already under construction in the Mitsubishi yard. However a fire in October 2005 so damaged her that *Sapphire Princess* was completed first, renamed *Diamond Princess*, and once the damaged vessel had been repaired and finished she was named *Sapphire Princess*. This enabled the company to minimise the marketing issues of a major delay to *Diamond Princess*.

In addition Princess also acquired three of the ships of the Renaissance Cruise Line that collapsed in 2001. *Minerva 2* (ex-*R8*) was transferred to Princess in 2007 to become *Royal Princess* whilst *R4* became *Tahitian Princess* and *R3* became *Pacific Princess* both in 2002. In mid-2008 it was announced that *Tahitian Princess* was to be renamed *Ocean Princess* in November 2009 to reflect her global cruising role. The 112,000 GRT *Ruby Princess* made her debut in 2008.

Above left: Artemis had a futuristic appearance when she entered service in 1984 as Royal Princess. (Roger Cartwright)

Above right: Royal Princess, now Artemis, approaches a set of locks on the Panama Canal. (Roger Cartwright)

Opposite top: Princess Rail carrying passengers bound for Whittier and their cruise ship. (Roger Cartwright)

Opposite bottom: The comfort of the Princess Rail dome cars en route from Fairbanks to Denali. (Roger Cartwright)

The original *Royal Princess* became *Artemis* in the UK fleet whilst *Crown Princess* joined the Ocean Village (see below) fleet as *Ocean Village 2* in 2007 after a stint in the German market as *A'rosa Blu*. *Regal Princess* became *Pacific Dawn* for P&O (Australia) in 2007.

PRINCESS IN ALASKA

Princess had been one of the first companies to expand into Alaska and P&O had used the *Arcadia* of 1954 in the area. Both Princess and Holland America expanded Alaska operations to include not only cruises but stays in their own lodges and even acquired their own sightseeing vehicles and trains. For the cruise passenger this meant a seamless means of seeing one of the last accessible wildernesses.

The Princess Alaskan operation is exceptionally well organised. Passengers have the options of just taking a cruise or adding on a Rocky Mountains or Alaskan land tour or indeed taking both land tours.

The Rocky Mountain land tours utilize the Rocky Mountaineer train between Jasper and Vancouver with a pre-train coach travel and an overnight stop in Kamloops between Jasper and Vancouver. The train enables passengers to experience the full grandeur of the Rocky Mountains.

In Alaska Princess offers a variety of land tours based on the five lodges that the company operates; Fairbanks, Denali, Mount McKinley, Copper River and Kenai Wilderness lodges. Each lodge comprises comfortable rooms, shops and a variety of diners and restaurants. Those feeling energetic can walk the trails surrounding the lodges and look out for bear, moose, bald eagles etc. The tours use buses and rail to transport passengers between the lodges. The whole exercise is an exemplar in logistics. Whether on a bus or a train before arriving at the next lodge the passenger receives an envelope containing details of the lodge they are travelling to, room keys and details of the next day's activities or journey.

Upon arriving in Alaska the passenger leaves a suitcase with Princess for the company to transfer to the ship and keeps another case for the land tour. This case is collected and delivered from the room in the lodge. Thus all the passenger needs to travel with is a hand tote and a camera.

The staff at the lodges are split between hotel staff and 'Princess Outfitters', the latter looking after transfers, excursions from the lodge etc.

The land tour case is delivered directly to the ship and on arrival in a stateroom the passenger finds their entire luggage waiting for them.

Check in for the cruise is undertaken on the final bus or train leg so that it is literally straight off the bus or train, through security and onto the ship.

Princess, Holland America, Celebrity and Royal Caribbean all operate their own train carriages. For the Fairbanks to Denali journey on the Denali Express all the companies' carriages operate in the same train pulled by Alaska Rail locomotives. The double-deck dome cars operated by Princess provide an upstairs seat for each passenger with a dining section in the lower portion of the carriage. On some journeys between Mt McKinley and the berth at Whittier single-deck panoramic cars converted by Alaska Rail from the stock of the Florida Fun Train are used. Due to the large-loading gauge of US railroads the view from these dome cars is superb. Each car has its own guide and bartender. It is difficult to imagine a more relaxing method of seeing Alaska. With control of the lodges and transportation, Princess is able to provide a seamless experience of guaranteed quality.

Right: The Princess Mount McKinley Wilderness Lodge. (Roger Cartwright)

Below: Diamond Princess and *Golden Princess* back to back in Skagway. (Roger Cartwright)

THE CARNIVAL COMES TO TOWN

When Ted Arison's Carnival Cruises' first vessel the *Mardi Gras* (the ex-Canadian Pacific Liner, *Empress of Canada*) left Miami on her maiden cruise in 1972, she went aground. It is reported that the company even named a drink after the incident: 'Mardi Gras on the Rocks'. Hardly an auspicious start for a new venture.

However, by 2003, Carnival was not only successful, it was the market leader in the fastest-growing sector of the tourism industry and poised to link up with P&O Princess.

Ted Arison had been a colonel in the Israeli Army and had then been involved in the air charter business. In 1966 he joined forces with a Norwegian, Knut Kloster, who had a new passenger ship, the *Sunward*, laid up in Europe. The cruise industry was just beginning to boom in the US and Arison suggested basing the *Sunward* at the then small port of Miami. Together Kloster and Arison formed Norwegian Caribbean Line (NCL), a company that became Norwegian Cruise Lines, eventually being owned by Star Cruises of Thailand.

NCL was very successful but in 1971 Arison and Kloster split up after financial disagreements. Kloster remained with NCL and Arison acquired the *Empress of Canada* and renamed her *Mardi Gras*. As mentioned earlier, the *Mardi Gras*'s first voyage in 1972 was marred by going aground but other maiden voyages and cruises have suffered mishaps (although none as great as the *Titanic*'s in 1912), P&O's new *Aurora* breaking down on her maiden cruise in 2000 being an example.

Arison grew Carnival by two means. The first was by offering a product to a new segment of the market – the younger holidaymaker – and secondly by acquiring well-known brands.

By 2001 Carnival Cruises operated over 1 million GRT of cruise ships in its own name but the Carnival Corporation is actually much larger.

The Carnival brand appeals to young, US vacationers, but of the 9.5 million people who undertook a cruise in 1999, many were neither young nor from the US. The UK is the second largest market and the rest of Europe provides another major slice. Many of those who enjoy cruises are older in years and the Carnival brand would not suit them. One of the best-known brands catering for the more mature vacationer is Holland America Cruises. Its ships are all in the premium price range and the cruises are less destination intensive than Carnival (Carnival ships typically stop at six destinations in seven days). Holland America has a very loyal customer base with high repeat business rates.

In 1987 Holland America acquired a 50 per cent stake in the Windstar Cruises (a company operating large sail-driven cruise ships) and completed the purchase the following year. However, later in 1988, Carnival acquired Holland America, giving it a foothold in the premier cruise market for more mature customers. Carnival changed very little. The appearance of Holland America ships, especially the livery, remained unchanged and they continued under their Dutch names and registry with little reference to the new ownership.

Above: Carnival Cruise's *Carnival Pride*. (Roger Cartwright)

Right: Small but beautifully formed, *Seabourne Pride* is also in the Carnival family. (Roger Cartwright)

Opposite: Rotterdam at Istanbul – Holland America is also a Carnival company. (Roger Cartwright)

In 1991 Carnival acquired a 25 per cent stake in the luxury operator Seabourn Cruises (operator of a series of small, yacht-like vessels). In 1996 Carnival purchased a 29.6 per cent stake in the UK vacation business of Airtours Plc at a cost of $310 million. Airtours were a very new entrant into the UK cruise market with an operation geared to the budget end of the market and linked to their core flights plus hotel package holidays. Airtours had a major stake in the Italian cruise company of Costa. Spending another $300 million in 1997, Carnival bought Costa Cruises in a shares plus cash deal with Airtours; Costa was a major player in both the US and European standard cruise markets. Airtours became independent of Carnival and the latter gained a valuable foothold in Southern Europe. Carnival also added one of the Club Med sailing cruise vessels to the Windstar fleet.

In the early years of the twentieth century the UK Government had kept Cunard (owners of some of the greatest Atlantic liners) out of the grasp of the US financier J.P. Morgan by providing subsidies on the stipulation that Cunard remained British. This changed in 1998 when Carnival acquired the Cunard cruise operation (including the *QE2*) and then built for Cunard what was briefly the world's largest ship, the *Queen Mary 2*.

By 2001 the acquisitions had added thirty-three ships plus four building with a combined tonnage of 1,492,000 GRT giving the Carnival Group forty-four ships totalling well over 2 million GRT. This made the Carnival Group easily the largest cruise conglomerate in the world with well over 33 per cent of the global market – a market that is still growing.

Below left: Costa is also a Carnival company – *Costa Fortuna* at Palma. (Roger Cartwright)

Below right: Cunard was acquired by Carnival in 1998. *QM2* is the Cunard flagship. (Roger Cartwright)

Carnival has expanded by acquiring traditional brands and keeping them very much as is. Indeed it is doubtful whether the customer knows they are actually on a Carnival-owned vessel.

It has not all been a success. Carnival had tried to acquire other operators, Premier Cruises and Royal Caribbean, but without success.

In 2003 talks were well underway for a merger between P&O Princess and Royal Caribbean. Then Carnival stepped in. The story is complex and involves not only the cruise companies but also the competition authorities in the UK, the European Union and the USA. Carnival won and P&O Princess joined the Carnival Group although its brands remained the same. There is an excellent telling of the Carnival and Princess story in *Devils on the Deep Blue Sea* by Kristopher A. Garin (see bibliography).

One advantage of being in the Carnival Group is the ability to acquire vessels from other members of the

Fireworks burst over the stern of *Ventura* after her naming by Dame Helen Mirren. (Mike O'Dwyer)

Group. As an example P&O's new *Arcadia* was laid down as *Queen Victoria* for Cunard and transferred to P&O whilst building (a new *Queen Victoria* was then built). A number of Carnival Group ships have been transferred to P&O (Australia). P&O Cruises was renamed Carnival plc London but the marketing was still under the P&O Cruises and Princess brands. One change to the P&O and Princess operation that might be noticed is the registry of the ships. P&O ships were always registered in London and flew the Red Ensign of the British Merchant Marine whilst Princess ships were either registered in London or Italy (reflecting the Sitmar connection). Today they are registered in the British Crown Colony of Bermuda and all fly the British Red Ensign. However, the captain of a ship registered in the UK cannot legally marry people, whilst if the ship is registered in Bermuda this restriction does not apply. Onboard weddings are very popular and a useful source of revenue – hence the ships are registered in Bermuda but still fly the British flag.

As mentioned earlier *Royal Princess* joined the UK fleet in 2005 as the adult-only ship *Artemis*. In that year *Adonia* went back to Princess under her old name of *Sea Princess* in 2005 although still catering for UK customers. In 2005 the adult-only *Arcadia* (laid down as *Queen Victoria*), at 83,000 GRT the largest British cruise ship ever at that time joined the fleet, followed in 2008 by the very large 115,000 GRT *Ventura* with another similar-sized ship building for 2010. *Ventura* (named after an area of California near to the Princess Cruises' HQ) is the largest vessel ever constructed for the UK cruise market. Whilst she enjoys many of the amenities common to the US market mega ships, her design and operation is rooted firmly in the UK tradition. The interior design by UK designer Nick Munro is extremely stylish, with artwork from

UK artists displayed throughout the ship. P&O Cruises has instituted a partnership with Tate Modern to provide talks and workshops etc. on contemporary art during cruises. With an impressive number of shops, a wide variety of entertainment venues and ten dining options plus balcony and in-cabin dining, *Ventura* is setting a standard for twenty-first-century UK cruising. She is a family oriented ship with a wide variety of dedicated activities for various age groups of children. For the first time on board a P&O Cruises' vessel there are dedicated facilities for the under two year olds, thus relieving the pressure on parents.

P&O Cruises prepared a set of 'fun facts' about the ship and (with their permission) these are reproduced below:

- The total number of passengers and crew on board Ventura – 4,296 – is enough to form 390 football teams.

- At 90,000bhp, Ventura's horsepower is equivalent to that of 190 Ferraris.

- 300 tonnes of paint are needed to paint Ventura, which is five times the amount of paint required to paint the Eiffel Tower.

- Ventura uses approximately 11 acres of carpet, enough to cover all the home grounds of the teams in the Six Nations.

- Ventura will travel approx 100,000 miles during her maiden season – the equivalent of circling the world more than four times.

- At 290 metres in length, Ventura is 22 metres longer than Tower Bridge.

- The picture mosaics in the centre stairwell contain more than 60,000 unique photos.

- Ventura is as long as thirty-five London buses or three football pitches laid end-to-end.

- Ventura also has the distinction of being possibly the only cruise ship with a model railway – installed in the Exchange bar and running for fifteen hours per day, even being able to cope with the ship listing.

A sister to *Ventura*, to be named *Azura*, is due to debut in 2010.

P&O DOWN UNDER

As its major Far East destination P&O (and Orient Line) has had a long relationship with Australia.

Australian cruising proper for the company began in 1974 when *Oriana* began to cruise out of both Sydney and Southampton, Sydney becoming her permanent base in 1981 until her withdrawal in 1986. She was joined between 1979 and 1982 by *Sea Princess*. P&O bought Sitmar in 1988 and the *Fairstar* continued her Australia-based cruises, begun in 1973 for her new owners. When she was withdrawn in 1997 her place was taken by *Fair Princess* (ex-*Fairsea* of Sitmar), a vessel that was actually a year older than the one she replaced. *Fairstar* was given an emotional send-off when she left Sydney for the last time – she had been a very popular ship. Sold in 2002 she was replaced by the *Sky Princess*, renamed *Pacific Sky*. As one of the last passenger vessels to be powered by steam turbines, she was disposed of to Pullmantur, Royal Caribbean's Spanish subsidiary, in 2006 to become *Sky Wonder*. There she joined another ex-Princess vessel, the *Pacific Princess*, one of the original Love Boats®.

Sapphire Princess in classic P&O territory – Circular Quay, Sydney. (Roger Cartwright)

Tropicale was the first new build for Carnival, delivered in 1981 as the first of a family of identical vessels. She was transferred Costa as *Costa Tropicale* in 2001 with her trademark funnel removed and replaced with the characteristic Costa funnel. In 2005 Carnival Group transferred *Costa Tropicale* to P&O (Australia) where she was renamed *Pacific Star*. In 2008 she was due to be based in Singapore, however, she was sold to Royal Caribbean-owned Pullmantur as *Ocean Dream*, for 2008 delivery. The big cruise groups do not usually sell ships to their rivals but this was the second sale to Pullmantur (*Sky Wonder* being the first at around the time Royal Caribbean acquired Pullmantur).

A larger version of *Tropicale*, *Jubilee* was transferred to P&O (Australia) in 2004 as *Pacific Sun*.

In 2007 *Regal Princess* was transferred to P&O (Australia) to become *Pacific Dawn* to operate alongside *Pacific Sun*. These two ships, at 70,000 GRT and 47,000 GRT respectively, comprise the 2008 fleet of P&O (Australia). In addition, in 2008 both *Sun Princess* and *Sapphire Princess* were operating regular cruises out of Australian ports.

A GERMAN INTERLUDE

The Verdi lips of *AidaVita*.
(Roger Cartwright)

P&O formed the German-based A'rosa Cruises in 1999 in association with Arkoma Cruises. Arkoma was a small operator with just two ships. *Crown Princess* was transferred to A'rosa Cruises in 2002 and received the name *A'rosa Blu*. *Regal Princess* was supposed to be transferred to this company, but this idea was dropped. When P&O Princess itself was acquired by Carnival Corporation in 2003 the A'rosa brand was discontinued. *A'rosa Blu* transferred to the German Aida Cruises as *Aida Blu*. P&O continued to market Aida until 2003 when the operation was transferred to Costa. The A'rosa and Aida (with the Verdi eyes and lips on its ships) product was a club-type operation and this made the *Aida Blu* ideal for conversion to *Ocean Village 2*.

OCEAN VILLAGE

A new P&O Cruise venture for the UK market was introduced in 2003. Branded as Ocean Village Cruises the concept was designed for the 'under forties, dress-down Fridays' generation who had not previously featured greatly in the UK market. Buffet meals, longer stays in ports, shorter seven-day cruises in the Mediterranean initially and even a supply of mountain bicycles were prominent features.

The first vessel, *Ocean Village*, was the *Arcadia* (ex-*Star Princess*) and she proved very successful in this role. She began to attract her own following and that has grown to include families and older customers. The operation was expanded to include the Caribbean in addition to the Mediterranean.

In spring 2007 a second ship was added, *Aida Blu*, ex-*Crown Princess*, ex-*A'rosa Blu*. She was an ideal choice as she had already been converted to a club-style ship.

Ocean Village, ex-Arcadia, ex-Star Princess at Rhodes in 2007. (Roger Cartwright)

Rising fuel costs during 2008 prompted an announcement in October of that year that the Ocean Village brand would be discontinued commencing in 2009 with *Ocean Village 2* moving to P&O Australia in late 2009 with *Ocean Village* herself following in 2010.

THE FUTURE

P&O were the originators of ocean cruising. Today in 2008 P&O Cruises, Princess and P&O (Australia) are still at the forefront of the industry. Now part of the giant Carnival Group the fleets have been expanded and modernised.

2008 saw the start of a downturn in the global economy with a credit crunch and a fall in property prices coupled to unprecedented prices for oil. A decline in customer confidence and increased costs will have an impact on the cruise industry. In 2001 the terrorist attacks on the USA led to the collapse of Premier Cruises, Renaissance Cruises and Festival Cruises (a company P&O nearly acquired). In 2008 the UK cruise operator Travelscope went out of business.

With the wealth of experience within P&O Princess and a modern fleet it is both hoped and expected that the P&O Cruises and Princess brands will weather the financial storms and still be sailing the seas in 2034, the 200th anniversary of Wilcox and Anderson's first venture, and taking a wider and wider customer base from the US, the UK, Canada and Australasia to more and more exciting destinations.

PART 2

Details of ships that have sailed for P&O companies

Ships are listed alphabetically. Details are given under the name carried by the ship when it first entered P&O service. For example the *Victoria* entered service as the *Sea Princess* and details will be found under the *Sea Princess* heading with a cross reference from the *Victoria* heading.

The number of cruise passengers stated is that normally carried and excludes extra pull-down berths that can accommodate two or three children in a two-berth cabin.

Adonia entering Honningsvag. She has now reverted to her *Sea Princess* name. (Roger Cartwright)

ADONIA – see SEA PRINCESS (1998)

AIDAaura

AIDA Cruises
42,280 GRT
Built in 2003 by Aker MTW (Germany)
1,266 passengers

A sister ship to *AIDAvita*, *AIDAaura* operates as a casual ship within the German cruise market. Like all the Aida Cruises ships she sports the red lips and blue eyes from Verdi's Aida – now under the Costa organisation following Costa acquisition of the Aida brand in 2004.

AIDA BLU – see CROWN PRINCESS/OCEAN VILLAGE 2

AIDAcara

AIDA Cruises
38,600 GRT
Built inw 1996 by Kvaerner Masa (Finland)
1,186 passengers

Originally named *Aida* until 2001. Operates as a casual ship within the German cruise market. Like all the Aida Cruises ships she sports the red lips and blue eyes from Verdi's Aida – now under the Costa organisation following Costa acquisition of the Aida brand in 2004.

AIDAvita

AIDA Cruises
42,280 GRT
Built in 2002 by Aker MTW Germany)
1,266 passengers

A sister ship to *AIDAaura*. *AIDAvita* operates as a casual ship within the German cruise market. Like all the Aida Cruises ships she sports the red lips and blue eyes from Verdi's Aida – now under the Costa organisation following Costa acquisition of the Aida brand in 2004.

ARCADIA (1954)

P&O Cruises
29,871 GRT
Built in 1953 by John Brown, Clydebank
1,400 passengers

Intended for the UK-Australia service the *Arcadia* and her near sister, *Iberia*, began to cruise more intensively in the late 1950s and early 1960s. They not only operated cruises for the UK market but were also based in San Francisco for cruises intended for the US market. In 1963 she was modernised in order to undertake more cruising. Between 1975 and her scrapping on Taiwan in 1979, *Arcadia* was employed solely on cruising.

ARCADIA (1997) – see STAR PRINCESS

ARCADIA (2005)

P&O Cruises
85,000 GRT
Built in 2005 by Fincantieri
1,996 passengers

Laid down as the *Queen Victoria* for Cunard she was transferred by Carnival from the Cunard operation to the P&O Princess brand whilst building. She was the largest cruise ship ever to be built for the UK market. She is of a similar design to other Carnival Group Vista Class vessels such as the *Carnival Spirit* and *Costa Atlantica*.

AROSA BLU – see CROWN PRINCESS

ARTEMIS (2005) – see ROYAL PRINCESS

Above: Arcadia – a classic P&O liner and popular cruise ship. (Painting by Robert Lloyd)

Left: The *Arcadia* of 2005 makes her maiden entry into Venice. (P&O)

Artemis, ex-*Royal Princess*, at Barcelona. (Roger Cartwright)

ASTORIA/ARKONA

AIDA Cruises
18,591 GRT
Built in 1981 by
Howaldtswerke – Deutsche
Weft AG (Hamburg)
500 passengers

Built for the German Cruise company Hadag Cruises her entry into service was delayed by fire. She was unsuccessful, having incurred huge losses in her first two years of service. In 1984 she was sold to South Africa for cruising and liner voyages from the UK to South Africa. She proved to be underpowered for the latter role. In 1985 she was transferred to the then East Germany to offer cruises for both East German workers and also Western tourists. She was renamed *Arkona*. The South Africans then ordered a very similar but with more powerful engines to become the new *Astor*. Following the re-unification of Germany she was acquired by Seetours. Renamed *Astoria* she remained with Seetours (which became Aida Cruises) until 2002 when she was sold to Transocean Tours who also operate the 1985 *Astor*. She is one of the few ships to have dialysis facilities on board.

AURORA

P&O Cruises
76,152 GRT
Built in 2000 by Meyer Weft,
Papenburg, Germany
1,870 passengers

So successful was *Oriana* and so bouyant was the UK cruise market in the late 1990s that P&O ordered a second vessel from the Meyer Weft yard. The new ship, *Aurora*, was to a similar but slightly larger design than *Oriana*. *Aurora*, only the second ship purpose built for a purely UK market, made her debut in May 2000. Launched by Princess Anne, she was only a few hours into her maiden cruise when a bearing went and the ship had to return to Southampton and the cruise was cancelled. It is a

Above: Aurora, Oriana's bigger sister. (Clive Harvey)

Below left: Classic sun terraces on *Aurora.* (Roger Cartwright)

Below right: Aurora has two double-deck penthouse suites right forward underneath the bridge. (Roger Cartwright)

measure of the way P&O handled the situation by keeping passengers informed and offering full refunds and a cruise that the mishap was turned from a potential public relations disaster into a triumph.

Aurora has had an interesting and successful career. She made her maiden entry into New York a few days before the 11 September attacks in 2001 and was at the centre of a series of diplomatic rows in 2004 when passengers were denied entry into Greece and the Spanish Government shut the border with Gibraltar when the ship docked there due to an outbreak of the Norwark virus that affected a minority of passengers. *Aurora* has undertaken a number of highly successful world cruises and has proved to be a very popular ship that is both modern and traditional. Her success was somewhat muted by events in January 2005 when her world cruise was delayed by days due to an engine problem. The passengers were accommodated on board and entertainment by top artists provided. Repairs in Southampton proved impossible and the cruise was cancelled at an estimated cost of £26 million.

CANBERRA

Canberra flying her paying
off pennant after arriving in
Southampton at the end of her
final cruise. (Clive Harvey)

P&O / P&O Cruises
44,807 GRT
Built in 1961 by Harland &
Wolff, Belfast
1,399 passengers

Canberra became possibly the best known British cruise ship.

Canberra and her running mate the *Oriana* of 1960 looked very different and yet were intended to operate on the same service.

A popular ship from her first voyage, *Canberra* had her share of mishaps, one of the most notable being on 4 January 1963 whilst she was off the southern Italian coast. A fire put the main engines out of action and there were no injuries amongst her 2,200 passengers. *Stratheden* was in the vicinity and provided assistance. In June 1967 she narrowly avoided being trapped in the Suez Canal on the outbreak of the Six-Day War. The ship was approaching Port Said when the staff captain heard a commercial radio report that Israeli aircraft were bombing Port Said. *Canberra* turned around and proceeded to take the long way around the Cape of Good Hope to Australia.

In 1973 *Canberra* commenced a series of cruises for the US market but she was not a success, in part due to her two-class nature; a division of facilities that was unacceptable to the US market.

Late in 1973 it was announced that *Canberra* was to be withdrawn and that *Orsova* and *Oriana* would operate the UK market cruises for P&O. *Canberra*'s draft was slightly greater than that of *Oriana* and it was believed that latter would be able to enter more ports. The conversion of *Orsova* to a one-class ship was, however, deemed too costly and *Canberra* was reprieved, refitted as a one-class ship in 1974 with accommodation for 1641 cruise passengers and gave over twenty years more service in the UK cruise market.

Canberra was allocated to the slowly re-emerging UK market where, throughout the 1970s, she built up a loyal following both for her normal two-week cruises out of Southampton and her annual world cruise that commenced in January for nearly three months.

In the spring of 1982 following the completion of her world cruise and a hasty survey on the final Gibraltar-Southampton leg of that cruise, 'The Great White Whale' as the Royal Navy nicknamed her was hastily converted to a troopship to carry 3 Brigade comprising elements of the Royal Marines and the Parachute Regiment to San Carlos Water in the Falklands Islands. Equipped with extensive medical facilities and helicopter landing pads, *Canberra* was in the first wave of the assault to recapture the Falkland Islands from the Argentines. Despite her conspicuous white appearance (she was never repainted grey) and her vast bulk she was not hit despite

Canberra berths after her final cruise. (Clive Harvey)

intensive Argentinean Air Force activity having spent three nerve-wracking days in the confined anchorage.

The British public had watched as *Canberra* had sailed out of the Solent on 9 April 1982 and they had cheered when she returned undamaged.

Canberra built up a tremendous loyalty amongst many of her passengers. By 1987 the ship had captured 20 per cent of all cruises sold in the UK and a massive 45 per cent of all cruises that originated in UK ports. Despite the fact that she still had many inside cabins, no balconies and a proportion of cabins without en suite facilities, *Canberra* was still holding market share well into the early 1990s with a regular 60 per cent repeat business complement of cruise passengers.

As a brand P&O Cruises was launched in 1988 based on *Canberra* and the smaller *Sea Princess* (later renamed *Victoria*). Also in that year, P&O decided to investigate either a new running mate or a replacement for *Canberra*. As it turned out, *Canberra* operated for a short period with the new ship, the *Oriana*, before being replaced by the 63,500-ton *Star Princess* transferred from the Princess operation and renamed *Arcadia*.

P&O Cruises was keen to retain the success of *Canberra* and went to great lengths to analyse why the ship had such a loyal following. This information was fed into the design of the *Oriana* of 1995.

Canberra's last cruise in the autumn of 1997 was emotional and the crowds thronged vantage points overlooking Southampton Water and the Solent to witness the last arrival and final departure of this much loved and highly influential ship. *Canberra* was broken up in Pakistan late in 1997 but her memory lingers on in the design of *Oriana* and *Aurora* and in the loyal *Canberra* passengers who can still be found on nearly every P&O cruise.

CARIBBEAN PRINCESS

Princess Cruises
116,000 GRT
Built in 2004 by Fincantieri (Italy)
3,114 passengers

A development of the Grand Princess class, she carries the jet engine-style pods on the funnel first introduced on *Coral Princess*. She was designed to operate year round in the Caribbean. Previously Princess Cruises had not operated in the Caribbean during the hurricane season. She is one deck higher than the Grand Princess ships and can thus carry a maximum of 3,782 passengers if all berths are occupied. Her normal capacity based on two passengers per cabin is 3,114. *Ventura* of the UK-based P&O Cruise fleet is to a similar design.

CHIMBORAZO

Orient Line
3,847 GRT
Built in 1871 by John Elder &
Co., Glasgow
72 first, 92 second, 265 third
class passengers

Chimborazo was designed for the Pacific Steam Navigation Company's South American service but was chartered in 1877 and then bought outright by Orient Line in 1878 for the Australia service. From 1891 she was used in the summer for cruising in Norwegian waters and the Mediterranean. She was sold in 1894 to a shipbroker and renamed *Cleopatra*. In 1895 she was sold to the Ocean Cruising & Highland Yachting Co. who only owned her until 1897 when she was broken up at Preston, Lancashire.

CHUSAN

P&O
24,318 GRT
Built in 1949 by Vickers
Armstrong, Barrow-in-Furness
464 first class & 541 tourist
class passengers

Only two years old, *Chusan* was used as an advertising poster for P&O's cruise operation in 1952. In the foreground is an oxen-powered sledge together with a native of Madeira (a favourite port of call then and now for UK cruise passengers). *Chusan*, with her white hull and yellow funnel, sits majestically in the background bathed in sunlight.

Chusan spent her whole career with P&O both on the liner routes to the Far East and Australia and as a popular cruise vessel for the UK market. In 1959 she undertook P&O's first world cruise covering 32,000 miles in eighty days and making stops at twenty-four ports. In 1970 *Chusan* operated the final P&O voyage to India, severing a link that had lasted over 100 years. Like so many other fine ships she was broken up in the early 1970s – in *Chusan*'s case in Taiwan in 1973.

CORAL PRINCESS

Princess Cruises
91,627 GRT
Built in 2002 by Chantiers de
l'Atlantique
1,974 passengers

In addition to building the large *Grand Princess* ships, Princess also decided to order two vessels midway in size between the *Dawn Princess* class and the *Grand Princess* class. These two vessels were named *Coral Princess* and *Island Princess*. Very modern in appearance they feature jet engine pods on the funnels. Both ships have a similar layout to the *Grand Princess* ships. Being slightly smaller they can transit the Panama Canal.

The striking 'jet engines' on the funnel of *Coral Princess*. (Roger Cartwright)

*Ocean Village 2, ex-Aida Blu,
ex-Crown Princess at Tortola.
(Roger Cartwright)*

CROWN PRINCESS (1990)

**Princess Cruises/A'rosa
Cruises/Aida Cruises/Ocean
Village 2**
70,285 GRT
Built in 1990 by Fincantieri
1,664 passengers

Crown Princess and her sister *Regal Princess* were ordered by Sitmar prior to the 1988 takeover by P&O. The largest P&O vessels up to that date, they present a striking appearance with the area over the bridge designed to resemble a dolphin.

Crown Princess sailed under the Princess brand until 2002 when she was transferred to the German market and the A'rosa brand as *A'rosa Blu*. The A'rosa operation was merged into the Aida brand in 2004 and the ship renamed *Aida Blu*. *Regal Princess* was to become the second of the Ocean Village vessels but, as *Aida Blu* had already been converted to a club-style format, it was announced in 2005 that she and not *Regal Princess* would be transferred to the Ocean Village operation as *Ocean Village 2* in 2007. She will relocate to the P&O Australia operation in 2009.

CROWN PRINCESS

Princess Cruises
113,651 GRT
Built in 2006 by Fincantieri
3,599 passengers
Sister to *Emerald Princess*

CUZCO

Orient Line
3,898 GRT
Built in 1871 by John Elder &
Co, Glasgow
70 first, 92 second, 228 third
class passengers

A sister of Chimborazo, *Cuzco was* designed for the PSNCo South American service but was chartered in 1877 and then bought outright by Orient Line in 1878 for the Australia service. She was switched to full-time cruising in 1902. In 1905 she was withdrawn and sold to Italian ship breakers.

The classic lines of an ex-Cunarder – *Dawn Princess* at anchor. (Clive Harvey)

DAWN PRINCESS (1988)

Princess Cruises
24,803 GRT
Built in 1956 by John Brown
906 passengers

Laid down as the *Sylvania* for Cunard's UK-Canada service, her career was cut short by the boom in transatlantic airliner operations. In 1968 she was sold together with her sister *Carinthia* to Sitmar and reamed *Fairwind*. Her other two sisters later went to Russian owners. Extensively refitted she was renamed *Sitmar Fairwind* in 1988 and became the only Sitmar vessel to carry the company's new livery due to the sale of Sitmar that year to P&O. She was allocated to the Princess brand as *Dawn Princess*. By 1993 she was surplus to requirements and was bought by Happy Days Shipping, a company that had major links with V ships – the Vlasov Group, the owners of Sitmar who had been her second owners. Chartered by Phoenix Seereisen of Germany as the *Albatros* (sic), she remained in service, a grand old veteran until 2004 when she was sold for scrap.

A study in sterns UK and US style – *Aurora* and *Dawn Princess* at Tortola. (Clive Harvey)

DAWN PRINCESS (1997)

Princess Cruises
77,500 GRT
Built in 1997 by Fincantieri
1,950 passengers

One of a class of four identical vessels. Of fairly conventional design and quite elegant appearance. Two of the class, *Ocean Princess* and *Sea Princess*, were transferred to the UK market as P&O Cruise's ships – *Ocean Princess* becoming *Oceana* and *Sea Princess* being renamed *Adonia*. In 2005 *Adonia* reverted to Princess Cruises and became *Sea Princess* again but marketed to a UK customer base.

DEVONIA

British India
12,796 GRT
Built in 1939 by Fairfield
shipbuilding & Engineering Co.
Ltd, Glasgow
194 cabin class passengers &
834 pupils

Entering service as the troopship *Devonshire* for Bibby Line she was a half-sister to the *Dunera*. Following the success of *Dunera* as an educational cruise ship, British India bought the *Devonshire* at the end of 1961 after it had been announced that the Government would in future move troops by air rather than by sea. Renamed *Devonia*, she was refitted by Barclay Curle in early 1962, entering educational cruise service in April. She sailed for British India carrying 194 cabin class passengers and 834 children for five years before being sold for scrap in Spain in December 1967.

The view from the bridge as *Diamond Princess* manoeuvres in Glacier Bay.

DIAMOND PRINCESS

Princess Cruises
115,875 GRT
Built in 2004 by Mitsubishi
2,674 passengers

Very similar to *Caribbean Princess*, *Diamond Princess* was to be the lead ship of an enlarged *Grand Princess* type. Whilst under construction in Japan a fire broke out, delaying completion. In order to keep to schedule, *Sapphire Princess*, her sister also completing in the same yard, was renamed *Diamond Princess* with the original *Diamond Princess* becoming *Sapphire Princess*.

DUNERA

British India
12,620 GRT
Built in 1937 by Barclay Curle &
Co. Ltd, Glasgow
187 cabin class passengers
& 834 pupils

Dunera was built as a troopship and as such was able to carry 1,150 troops, as well as 3,400 tons of cargo. *Dunera* operated just one season of pre-war school cruising, during the summer of 1939. Between March 1950 and March 1951 her accommodation was modernised by her builders, and she was then employed for a further ten years in trooping duties. Released from this service early in 1961, following the decision by British India to re-enter educational cruising, she was converted into a full-time educational cruising ship, fitted with six classrooms. She could accommodate 187 cabin class passengers and 834 children. She made fifteen educational cruises in her first year, and the experiment was such a success that she carried 9,704 passengers in that period. The success of *Dunera* in this role was such that three further British India ships were also converted for educational cruising roles. She remained in service until November 1967, when she was scrapped in Spain.

The crew on *Diamond Princess* have facilities that rival those for the passengers on older ships. (Roger Cartwright)

EMERALD PRINCESS

Princess Cruises
116,000 GRT
Ordered from Fincantieri (Italy)
in 2005.
3,100 cruise passengers

Part of a four-ship Carnival Corporation order that included *Ventura* for the UK market.

FAIR PRINCESS

Princess Cruises / P&O Holidays (Australia)
24,803 GRT
Built in 1956 by John Brown
906 passengers

Like her sister *Sylvania* (later *Dawn Princess*) she was designed for Cunard's UK-Canada service and named *Carinthia* but her career was cut short by the boom in transatlantic airliner operations. In 1968 she was sold together with her sister *Sylvania* to Sitmar and renamed *Fairland*. Her other two sisters later went to Russian owners. Extensively refitted, she was renamed *Fairsea* in 1971. Following the sale of Sitmar in 1988 to P&O she was allocated to the Princess brand as *Fair Princess*. From 1998 she operated in the Far East for P&O (Australia) replacing the *Fairstar*. In 2000 her sale as a Hong Kong-based casino / cruise ship to Canadian / Chinese interests was announced.

Renamed *China Sea Discovery*, she was placed on four-day, three-night cruises to Haikou, Hainan Island, then to Halong Bay in Vietnam. On her maiden voyage, she went aground twice, due to her 29ft draft – hardly an auspicious start to a new career. She returned to Hong Kong and commenced overnight gambling cruises. This venture was also a failure – there were at least with seven other ships, most of which were in far better condition, operating the same type of overnight gambling cruises. She was consequently relocated to Keelung, Taiwan, but continued to lose money. She was laid up in Kaohsiang on 21 May 2003, forlornly awaiting a buyer or the breakers yard, before sailing for scrapping in India in 2005.

Emerald Princess berthed in Istanbul. (Roger Cartwright)

FAIRSTAR

P&O Holidays (Australia)
23,764 GRT
Built in 1957 by Fairfield
Shipbuilding (UK)
1,300 passengers

Built as the troopship *Oxfordshire* for Bibby Line, she was sold to Sitmar in 1963. Sitmar operated her on the UK-Australia liner service. She commenced her full-time cruising career in 1973 being based in Sydney. Transferred to P&O after the sale of Sitmar in 1988 she retained her name and operated the P&O Holidays Australia market cruises until replaced by *Fair Princess* in 1997. A popular 'fun' ship despite some well-publicised breakdowns, she found no further employment and sailed for scrapping with the temporary name *Ripa* on 12 February 1997. It should be noted that the replacement, *Fair Princess*, was actually the older vessel!

Fair Princess proclaims her P&O ownership. (Clive Harvey)

GARONNE

Orient Line
3,876 GRT
Built in 1878 by Napier & Sons,
Glasgow
60 first, 100 second, 320 third
class passengers

Build for the Pacific Steam Navigation Company (PSNC) in 1871, *Garonne* was an elegant ship complete with auxiliary sails and a bowsprit. She was chartered from PSNC for the London-Melbourne service in 1877 and purchased outright for £71,570 in 1878. By 1897 the ship had completed twenty-five mail voyages to Australia and forty-one cruises. From 1889 she was employed almost exclusively in the cruise market.

Sold in 1897 she carried prospectors to the Klondike for the gold rush and then served the US Government as a troopship in the Spanish American War of 1898. She was scrapped in Genoa in 1905.

Far left: Simple elegance on board *Fair Princess*. (Clive Harvey)

Left: Comfort at sea – an outside twin cabin on *Fair Princess*. (Clive Harvey)

The distinctive 'shopping trolley' stern of *Golden Princess*. (Roger Cartwright)

GOLDEN PRINCESS (1993)

Princess Cruises
28,078 GRT
Built in 1972 by Wartsila (Finland)
867 passengers

One of three 21,800 GRT sisters built for the Royal Viking Line, she was 'stretched' in 1983. She was sold to Norwegian Cruise Line (NCL) in 1984 but continued to sail under her original name and brand until 1991 when she was renamed *Sunward*. Sold to Birka as the *Birka Queen* she was chartered by Princess Cruises in June 1993 as a replacement for *Dawn Princess*, remaining in Princess service until 1996. She then became the Superstar *Capricorn* of Star Cruises (later to become the owners of NCL). A very brief spell as the *Hyundai Keumgang* followed before she reverted to Star Cruises. In 2004 she was chartered to the Spanish Viajes Ibrejet cruise company. This too was to be a short career as in 2005 it was announced that Fred Olsen Cruises had acquired her to join her ex-sister *Royal Viking Star*, by then operating as the *Black Watch*, renaming her *Boudicca*.

GOLDEN PRINCESS (2001)

Princess Cruises
108,685 GRT
Built in 2001 by Fincantieri
2,600 passengers

The second of the *Grand Princess* class to enter service and, like her sisters, too wide for the Panama Canal.

GRAND PRINCESS

Princess Cruises
108,806 GRT
Built in 1998 by Fincantieri
2,600 passengers

The lead ship of three 'mega-ships' all too wide for the Panama Canal. The ships also possess a 'spoiler' attached to the stern that holds an aft-facing observation lounge. The three ships were the Princess answer to the huge 100,000+ GRT cruise liners introduced by Carnival Cruise from 1996 onwards before the Carnival-P&O / Princess merger. From 2009 she is scheduled to replace *Sea Princess* in the UK market.

HIMALAYA

P&O
28,047 GRT
Built in 1948 by Vickers
Armstrong, Barrow-in-Furness
1,416 tourist class passengers

P&O's first post-war ship the *Himalaya* operated as a two-class ship on the UK-India-Australia liner service.

In 1963 she was refitted as a tourist class vessel and as air travel began to eat into the liner trade, *Himalaya* undertook more and more cruises. Her cruising career paralleled that of ships like the *Orcades* whom she was built next to in the same yard. She was broken up in Taiwan in 1974.

IBERIA

P&O
29,614 GRT
Built in 1954 by Harland &
Wolff, Belfast
673 first class & 733 tourist
class passengers

Like her semi-sister *Arcadia*, she was built for the UK-Australia service in addition to cruising. Never as popular as *Arcadia*, she was scrapped in Taiwan in 1972, seven years before *Arcadia* was withdrawn.

ISLAND PRINCESS (1974)

Princess Cruises
19,907 GRT
Built in 1971 by Rheinstahl
Nordseewerke (Emden)
767 passengers

Together with her sister ship, *Pacific Princess*, she was a ship that may have been responsible more than any other for introducing people to cruising. Owned by Flagship Cruises and originally named *Island Venture*, she became *Island Princess* and was part of the small Princess Cruise fleet of Stanley B. McDonald. She was acquired together with *Pacific Princess* and the Princess operation by P&O in 1974. Both ships became the stars of the highly popular *The Love Boat*® television series and appeared on millions of television sets both in North America and the UK weekly.

In 1999 she was sold to become firstly the *Hyundai Pungak* and then the *Platinum* before becoming the *Discovery* of Voyages of Discovery in 2003.

The promenade deck of *Discovery*, ex-*Island Princess*. (Roger Cartwright)

ISLAND PRINCESS (2002)

Princess Cruises
91,627 GRT
Built in 2003 by Chantiers de
l'Atlantique
1,974 passengers

Sister ship to *Coral Princess*, she entered service in December 2002. Both ships have a similar layout to the *Grand Princess* ships. Being slightly smaller, both can transit the Panama Canal.

LUSITANIA

Orient Line
85 first, 100 second & 270
third class passengers
3,877 GRT
Built in 1878 by Laird Brothers,
Birkenhead.

Similar in appearance to the *Garonne*, the Orient Line *Lusitania* is less well known than the Cunard liner of 1907 of the same name that was torpedoed with great loss of life in 1915.

Lusitania was designed for the PSNCo South American service but like *Garonne* was chartered and then bought outright by Orient Line for the Australia service. In 1882 and again in 1884 she was chartered by the Government firstly as a troopship and latterly as an Armed Merchant Cruiser (AMC).

Following her military service she was refitted in 1886 and was then chartered to PSNCo until 1893. Returned to Orient Line she made her last mail sailing in 1897.

From 1897 until 1889 she cruised exclusively until in August 1899 she collided with a jetty in Copenhagen. Orient Line desired to replace the ship and she was sold to Elder Dempster Line for £15,000 and placed on the Beaver Line service to Canada.

Below left: Island Princess now sails as the Discovery for Voyages of Discovery. (Roger Cartwright)

Below right: Minerva 2 now the new Royal Princess. (Clive Harvey)

MINERVA

Swan Hellenic
12,000 GRT
Built in 1996 by Marriotti (see
note below)
456 passengers

Minerva was laid down as the *Okean* – a spy ship for the Soviet Navy. The incomplete hull was purchased by the V Ships concern (V Ships had connections to Sitmar Line in the past and also to Silversea Cruises). The ship was completed in Italy and was especially tailored to the needs of Swan Hellenic. She gained a reputation for elegance and culture. Her library was one of the best afloat. So popular were the Swan Hellenic cruises that the need for a larger vessel became apparent and in 2002 it was announced that she was to be chartered by Saga Cruises as the *Saga Pearl* for six months of the year and by Abercrombie and Kent as the *Explorer* for the other six months. In November 2004 she made her last voyage for Saga – a cruise to Brazil. In 2005 she was chartered by Phoenix Reisen of Germany as the *Alexander von Humboldt*. When Carnival Group announced that it was discontinuing the Swan Hellenic brand, the brand was acquired by Lord Sterling who arranged to charter her from Voyages of Discovery (by now owned by the UK All Leisure Group) who had renamed her *Explorer 2* from 2008 onwards as a revitalised Swan Hellenic.

MINERVA II

Swan Hellenic/Princess Cruises
30,277 GRT
Built in 2001 by Chantiers de
l'Atlantique, France
700 passengers

The replacement for *Minerva* from 2004 onwards was the *Minerva II*. Built as the *R Eight* she was the last of the identical 'R' ships built for Renaissance Cruises between 1998 and 2001. Renaissance Cruises suffered heavily after 11 September 2001 and with the company in dire financial straits all of the ships were placed on the market. In addition to *R8*, P&O also acquired two more of these vessels for operating under the Princess brand in the Pacific – see *Tahitian Princess* and *Pacific Princess* (2002). In 2006 it was announced that she would leave the Swan Hellenic fleet to join her two sisters already operating for Princess Cruises as the new *Royal Princess* from 2007, thus giving the company three of the eight ex-Renaissance ships.

MOLDAVIA

P&O
16,436 GRT
Built in 1921 by Cammell
Laird, Birkenhead
830 passengers when cruising

Like her sister *Mongolia*, *Moldavia* was given a new lease of life in 1931 by being refitted as an 830-capacity tourist class / cruise ship. She spent her year either cruising or on the intermediate (as opposed to the express) service from UK to Australia. Being a tourist class-only ship her cruise fares were more affordable. She was broken up in the UK in 1938.

MONGOLIA

P&O
16,385 GRT
Built in 1922 by Armstrong
Whitworth, Walker-on-Tyne
830 passengers when cruising

Like her sister *Moldavia*, *Mongolia* was given a new lease of life in 1931 by being refitted as an 800 passenger tourist class / cruise ship. She spent her year either cruising or on the intermediate (as opposed to the express) service from UK-Australia. Being a tourist class only ship, her cruise fares were more affordable.

Mongolia was a long-lived ship. When she and her sister left P&O service she was not broken up like *Moldavia*. In 1938 she was chartered to the New Zealand Steamship Company for whom she traded as the *Rimutaka* until 1950. She was then sold on to continue trading until she scrapped in Japan in 1963.

NEURALIA

British India
9,082 GRT
Built in 1912 by Barclay Curle
& Co. Ltd, Glasgow
50 cabin class and up to 1,050
troops / pupils

Neuralia was the ship that introduced British India's educational cruises, in July 1932. After the First World War she had been placed on the London-East Africa service but from 1925 onward she was given over to permanent trooping duties. When not on trooping duties she was laid up. In 1932 *Neuralia* inaugurated the school ship cruises, which would eventually become extremely popular. *Neuralia*'s cruises took her up to the Baltic and the Norwegian fjords, and she continued these cruises when not on trooping duties until 1935. She sank in the Mediterranean in May 1945, having struck a mine off Taranto.

NEVASA

British India

20,746 GRT

Built in 1956 by Barclay Curle & Co. Ltd, Glasgow

308 cabin class passengers & 1,090 pupils

Nevasa entered service as a troopship with accommodation for 220 first class, 110 second class and 180 third class passengers and 1,000 troops. She was employed in this role for six years before it was decided that future troop movements would be undertaken by air rather than by sea. She was laid up in the River Fal in October 1962 at the end of her final trooping voyage. In 1964 *Nevasa* was sent to the shipyard of Silley Cox & Co. Ltd, to be given a £500,000 refit, transforming her into an educational cruise ship for 308 cabin class passengers and 1,090 children. *Nevasa* departed Southampton on 28 October 1965 on her first educational cruise, to Madeira, Tangier and Lisbon. Although her deep draft hull limited the range of ports that she could berth at she was nevertheless a very popular ship. Her career was brought to a premature end with the oil crisis (her engines were very thirsty) of the early 1970s, and she was sold to be scrapped in Taiwan in April 1975.

The British India educational cruise ship *Nevasa*. (Painting by Robert Lloyd)

The spacious wrap-around promenade deck of *Oceana* (ex *Ocean Princess*). (Roger Cartwright)

OCEAN VILLAGE – see ARCADIA (1997) / OCEAN VILLAGE

OCEAN VILLAGE 2 – see CROWN PRINCESS / A'ROSA BLU / AIDA BLU

OCEANA – see OCEAN PRINCESS

OCEAN PRINCESS (2000)

Princess Cruises/P&O Cruises
77,499 GRT
Built in 2000 by Fincantieri, Italy
1,950 passengers

A sister ship to *Dawn Princess*, *Sea Princess* and *Sun Princess*. With the disposal of *Victoria* and the re-branding of *Acadia* as *Ocean Village*, the *Ocean Princess* was transferred from the US to the UK P&O Princess operation in November 2002 and renamed *Oceana*. *Oceana* together with the slightly older *Adonia* (ex-*Sea Princess*) formed the two new 'White Sisters' reintroducing a term used for the *Strathaird* and the *Strathnaver* in the early 1930s.

Refitted to appeal to UK rather than US cruise passengers, the *Oceana* features the latest in cruise ship interior design with large atriums together with glass-walled lifts. Named by Princess Anne in a joint ceremony with Zara Phillips (Princess Anne's daughter) who named *Adonia*. The bottle did not break on *Oceana*'s bow but the ship does not seem to have suffered any bad luck as a result.

In the autumn of 2002 *Oceana* commenced her operations for the UK cruise market with a series of Caribbean cruises based on Fort Lauderdale in the USA before making her maiden entry to the UK in the spring of 2003.

Plenty of sunbathing space on *Ocean*'s (ex *Ocean Princess*') lido deck. (Roger Cartwright)

Oceana, ex-*Ocean Princess*. (Roger Cartwright)

OCEAN PRINCESS (2009) – see TAHITIAN PRINCESS

OPHIR

Orient Line

6,814 GRT

Built in 1891 by Robert Napier & Sons, Glasgow

230 first class, 142 second class & 520 steerage class passengers

Not many people have had the opportunity to cruise on a Royal Yacht but that was one of *Ophir*'s claims to fame. Built as the first twin-screw vessel on the Australian mail service, *Ophir* was refitted as a Royal Yacht for the visit of the Duke and Duchess of Cornwall and York (later King George V and Queen Mary) for their visit to Australia and New Zealand in 1901. The ship called at a number of other British possessions on both the outward and homeward journeys. From the summer of 1902 onwards she made regular cruises from the UK to the Norwegian fjords. A thirteen-day cruise to Norway in 1907 cost from 13 guineas – a not inconsiderable sum in those days!

In 1914 on the outbreak of war she was chartered by the Admiralty initially as a mail steamer (her normal roll) but then as an Armed Merchant Cruiser (AMC) from 1915 onwards. After service in the Far East she returned to the UK to pay off. She was retained by the Admiralty and finally sold for a mere £6,000 in 1922 for scrapping at Troon, Scotland, after lying idle since 1919.

ORAMA

Orient Line

19,840 GRT

Built in 1924 by John Brown & Co., Clydebank

982 passengers when cruising

The first of a group of five ships launched between 1924 and 1929 for the Australia mail service. She followed the pattern of line voyages to Australia and UK-based cruises to the Mediterranean and the Norwegian fjords. Her accommodation was changed to 484 first and 498 tourist in 1935, making her more acceptable as a cruise ship.

Her last pleasure cruise was out of Sydney in the summer of 1939 and by 12 December she was in Government service as a troopship. On 6 June 1940 she was in company with the hospital ship *Atlantis* proceeding to Narvik in Norway to evacuate troops when the German cruiser *Hipper* spotted them and her escorting destroyers. Respecting the conventions governing hospital ships, the *Atlantis* was allowed to proceed but the *Omara* was attacked in the belief that she was an Armed Merchant Cruiser. Fortunately she had no troops on board. Twenty members of her crew were killed whilst the rest were rescued by the German ships and spent the war in Stalag XIIIA.

ORCADES (1937)

Orient Line

23,456 GRT

Built in 1937 by Vickers
Armstrong, Barrow-in-Furness

486 first & 653 tourist class
passengers

The war cut short this ship's cruising career. A sister of *Orion* she undertook a series of cruises in 1938 but only one in 1939. She arrived back from the Mediterranean in April with an engine defect and was sent up to Barrow for repairs. She was requisitioned as a troopship after her repair and on the morning of 10 October 1942 she was torpedoed by *U172* whilst on passage between Cape Town and Freetown in West Africa with 1,300 service personnel and civilians on board. She survived the first attack but lowered her boats, one of which capsized with the loss of thirty-eight lives, but with the remainder of her passengers and many crew members safely picked up by the Polish steamer *Narvik* and was limping back to Cape Town. The captain and a skeleton crew of fifty-one volunteers were endeavouring to make port when the U-boat attacked again and three more torpedoes hit *Orcades*. Luckily the *Narvik* was still in the vicinity and, despite being a cargo vessel with a crew of only forty-seven, she brought nearly 1,700 survivors back to Cape Town. They had been very lucky, as the attack had occurred 300 miles from port.

ORCADES (1948)

Orient Line

28,472 GRT

Built in 1948 by Vickers
Armstrong, Barrow-in-Furness

770 first, 742 tourist class
passengers

The first of three similar vessels she commenced her cruise career in 1951. In 1959 she became the first Orient Line ship to be fitted with what is now the norm for cruise ships – air conditioning. As a result of the merger with P&O she joined the combined fleet and carried out regular cruises not only for the UK market but also for the Australian one. She was refitted as a one-class ship in 1964 with accommodation for 1,400 passengers. Her final years were spent cruising from Southampton where she was decommissioned in October 1972, reaching the breakers yard on Taiwan in February 1973.

ORFORD

Orient Line
19,941 GRT
Built in 1928 by Vickers,
Barrow-in-Furness
520 first, 1,162 third class
passengers

The fourth ship of the *Orama* type to enter service. She followed the pattern of line voyages to Australia and UK-based cruises to the Mediterranean and the Norwegian fjords. Like her sisters her accommodation was changed to 468 first and 515 tourist in 1935, making her more acceptable as a cruise ship.

Her career was cut short in 1940. She had been loaned to the French Government as a troopship together with *Otranto* and was tasked to transport troops from Madagascar to Marseilles. She arrived at the French port and whereas *Otranto* was sent to a secure base in the port, *Orford* was directed to an exposed anchorage. The Luftwaffe found her on 1 June 1940 and the subsequent bombing and sinking cost the lives of fourteen crew together with twenty-five injured. She was the first Orient Line vessel to be lost in the war.

ORIANA (1960)

P&O
41,920 GRT
Built in 1960 by Vickers
Armstrong, Barrow-in-Furness
638 first & 1,496 tourist
class passengers, 1,700 cruise
passengers from 1973

The last ship ordered by Orient Line before the whole of the company's shares were acquired by P&O. *Oriana* was intended, like *Canberra*, for the UK-Australia liner service. Dredging of the Suez Canal in the 1950s meant that 40,000 GRT ships could transit the canal.

Her original livery retained the corn-coloured Orient Line hull before she was repainted with a P&O white hull. From the outset she was also used for cruising and from 1973 onwards she was employed purely in the cruise trade, alternating between UK and Australian market cruises.

Of a striking design, *Oriana* was instantly recognisable. Considerable use of aluminium was made in her superstructure and she was one of earliest ships to be fitted with 'transverse propulsion units', known as bow thrusters, to aid docking manoeuvres.

Elegant throughout, the *Oriana* was very popular with her passengers and crew alike. The accommodation for the latter was the best that had ever been seen in a UK-registered ship up to that time. On 11 August 1970 she left berth 106 bound for Australia with 1,500 passengers on board. Only an hour into the voyage there was a serious boiler fire and the ship lost all power. Passengers were called to their emergency stations although an evacuation proved unnecessary. The fire burned for over an hour and with no power and in danger of grounding it might have taken hold and the ship could have been lost.

Laid down for the Orient Line, the *Oriana* of 1960 spent her final years cruising out of Australia. (Clive Harvey)

The *Oriana* of 1995 was the first purpose-built cruise ship dedicated to the UK market. (Roger Cartwright)

ORIANA (1995)

P&O Cruises
69,153 GRT
Built in 1995 by Meyer Weft,
Papenburg, Germany
1,828 cruise passengers

In 1973 it was announced that *Canberra* was to be withdrawn and that *Orsova* and *Oriana* would operate the UK market cruises for P&O. *Canberra*'s draft was slightly greater than that of *Oriana* and it was believed the latter would be able to enter more ports. The conversion of *Orsova* to a one-class ship was however deemed too costly and *Canberra* was reprieved, refitted as a one-class ship in 1974 and gave over twenty years more service in the UK cruise market.

By the early 1970s it was clear that the market for cruise passengers was moving rapidly in the direction of one-class ships. The US market led the field and UK operators were forced to follow suit. In 1973 *Oriana* was refitted as a one-class ship, reducing her capacity to 1,700 cruise passengers. This was so successful that in 1974 it was announced that all P&O cruise ships would be one-class.

In 1976 the scrapping of *Oronsay* meant that *Oriana* was the last of the Orient Line ships.

By the 1980s much of her cruising was in the Australian market but in 1986 she was sold to Japanese buyers for use as a museum ship in Beppu Bay, Japan. Later she was sold to China as a floating hotel and conference centre in Shanghai where she retained both her P&O livery and the name *Oriana*. In 2002 she was sold to the Port of Dalian in north-east China. She broke free from her moorings in a typhoon in late 2004 and was sold to Indian breakers in 2005.

By 1991 it was clear that *Canberra* would not be suitable for service into the latter years of the decade and an order was placed for the first ever purpose-built cruise liner for the UK cruising market. Whilst it was popularly believed that *Oriana* was a straight replacement for *Canberra* this was not the case as the ships operated alongside each other until September 1997 when *Canberra* was withdrawn and replaced by the *Arcadia* (ex-*Star Princess*).

No British yard felt able to compete for the order and it was gained by the experienced cruise liner building yard of Meyer Weft in Germany.

Designed by Robert Tillberg, who spent time on board *Canberra* whilst refining his ideas, *Oriana* is an extremely elegant ship and brought new standards of accommodation to the UK cruise market, including a whole deck of staterooms and suites with balconies. Unlike the US market ships where all cabins are referred to as staterooms, on *Oriana* and the later *Aurora* the term stateroom is reserved for a class of accommodation priced between that of standard cabins and mini-suites.

In 2002 *Oriana* was hit by a huge wave in mid-Atlantic. A number of windows were smashed. Reports suggest that the crew behaved in an exemplary manner but this did not stop the ship appearing on a 'Cruises from Hell' television programme. It appears that there was never any danger and passengers were compensated fully by P&O Cruises. *Oriana* has also undertaken annual world cruises in addition to her regular series of cruises to the traditional P&O destinations and the newer ones such as South America. From 2004 however the World Cruises were handled by *Aurora* and *Adonia* with *Oriana* joining *Oceana* in the Caribbean and South America during the UK winter season.

Oriana enters the Golden Horn from a Black Sea cruise, October 2008. (Roger Cartwright)

ORION

Orient Line
23,371 GRT
Built in 1934 by Vickers Armstrong, Barrow-in-Furness
486 first & 653 tourist class passengers

Orion was quite revolutionary, being the model for many subsequent liners with her single funnel and single mast. Her launch was also unique at the time as she was launched by HRH the Duke of Gloucester who was in Australia at the time and carried out the ceremony by radio.

With splendid interiors designed by the architect Brian O'Rorke, the ship moved away from the trend of making ships like land-based hotels and instead used the ship itself to create the ambience.

Like earlier Orient Line ships her Australia runs were punctuated with cruising from the UK in summer. In 1939, however, like so many other liners, she was requisitioned for war duties as a troopship. She was in Singapore when the Japanese attacked in September 1941 but after embarking wounded troops and civilian evacuees she arrived safely in Fremantle on 6 January 1942. Refitted at Barrow in 1947 she resumed her Australia sailings.

In June 1951 *Orion* commenced her first post-war cruise – thirteen nights to that favourite Orient Line destination – the Norwegian fjords. Fares ranged from £39 to £65. In 1953 she was placed on an Australia-Vancouver-San Francisco service but in 1958 she was converted to a one-class tourist ship for the emigrant trade from the UK to Australia.

With the merger with P&O in 1960, *Orion* was withdrawn from service in May 1963 flying an 84ft-long paying-off pennant as she steamed into the Thames Estuary. After a brief charter to a German company as a hotel ship she sailed for the breakers yard in Antwerp in October 1963.

Orion in heavy weather. (Painting by Robert Lloyd)

ORMONDE

Orient Line

14,981 GRT

Built in 1917 by John Brown & Co., Clydebank

700 passengers when cruising

Ormonde was laid down in 1913 but due to the war she was not completed until 1917 and then only because the need for ships was so great. Initially she was fitted out as a troopship and did not leave Government service until 1919.

She was the largest Orient Line vessel to that date. Her maiden voyage for the company was on the Australia mail service on 11 November 1919. Her first cruise was to the Norwegian fjords in the summer of 1922. In 1923 she was converted to a two-class ship and continued her series of Norwegian cruises. From the 13 guineas minimum fare in 1907 on *Ophir*, the same cruise was now 20 guineas.

She spent much of the time between 1924 and 1939 on the Australia service being converted to a one-class tourist ship in 1933 with accommodation for 700 passengers. By that time passengers were demanding more room!

In the late spring and early summer of 1939 she spent the season cruising the Norwegian fjords, leaving for Australia on 12 August. On her arrival back in the UK she was requisitioned as a troopship, a role she carried out with distinction throughout the war.

Converted to an 'austerity' liner for emigrant passengers in 1950 she was withdrawn in 1952 to be scrapped at Dalmuir, Scotland, only a few miles from where she had been launched thirty-five years before.

ORMUZ

Orient Line

14,588 GRT

Built in 1914 by Bremen Vulkan, Germany

292 first & 828 third class (no second class) passengers

Ormuz was one of three German liners handed over to the British Government as war reparations and purchased by Orient Line. Many British shipping companies had their sunken tonnage replaced with German vessels.

As the *Zeppelin*, *Ormuz* had been launched by Count Zeppelin (of airship fame) himself on 9 June 1914 and was intended to be one of a series of vessels for a Norddeutscher Lloyd NDL) service to Australia. She was still not completed when war broke out but was fitted out by 1915 and then laid up as there would have been no chance of her breaking the blockade the Royal Navy was maintaining against German commerce.

Initially after being handed over to Britain she was owned by the Shipping Controller and managed by the White Star Line. After a refit in 1920 she was purchased by the Orient Line and given her new name.

Her first role was to resume the Norwegian cruises, the first of which was undertaken in June 1921. She continued a mix of mail voyages to Australia and cruises from the UK until 1926 when she was withdrawn as being unsuitable for the Orient Line service.

She eventually ended up back in the hands of her original owners (NDL) in 1927, who paid a mere £25,700 for her. Renamed *Dresden* she became one of the pioneer 'Strength Through Joy' cruises initiated by the Nazi government and organized by Dr Robert Ley, the leader of the Labour Front in Germany. These cruises were designed as a low-cost opportunity for German workers to undertake cruising.

In June 1934 she struck an uncharted rock in Norwegian waters and sank. Fortunately all but three of her passengers and crew were saved.

ORONSAY (1925)

Orient Line
20,001 GRT
Built in 1925 by John Brown & Co., Clydebank
501 first & 482 second class passengers as a cruise ship

Oronsay followed the usual Orient Line pattern of line voyages to Australia and UK-based cruises to the Mediterranean and the Norwegian fjords. Her accommodation was reduced in 1935, making her more acceptable as a cruise ship.

Requisitioned as a troopship she was en route to the UK with only fifty passengers, mainly civilians, when she was torpedoed and sunk by the Italian submarine *Archimede* on 9 October 1942. The Royal Navy picked up 266 survivors with another boatload of survivors being picked up by another merchant ship.

ORONSAY (1951)

Orient Line/P&O
28,136 GRT
Built in 1948 by Vickers Armstrong, Barrow-in-Furness
668 first & 833 tourist class passengers – later one class only

The second new ship for the company after the war, *Oronsay*'s entry into service was delayed by a fire whilst fitting out – a mishap that has occurred to a number of other vessels. Undertaking a similar liner and cruise schedule to her sister *Orcades*, she was fitted with air conditioning in 1959. She was formerly transferred to P&O in 1964 and by 1972 she was operating solely as a one-class cruise ship although more from Australia than the UK. Her final UK cruise was from the UK to Madeira, the Canaries, Morocco, Gibraltar and Northern Spain in July / August 1975. She made one more trip to Sydney and then a final cruise to Hong Kong where she remained before sailing to the breakers yard in October 1975.

ORONTES

Orient Line/P&O
20,186 GRT
Built in 1929 by Vickers,
Barrow-in-Furness
463 first and 418 tourist
passengers as a cruise ship

The last of the *Orama* type. She followed the pattern of line voyages to Australia and UK-based cruises to the Mediterranean and the Norwegian fjords with occasional trips to the Caribbean. Her accommodation was reduced in 1935, making her more acceptable as a cruise ship.

Requisitioned as a troopship she survived the war and resumed her commercial sailings in 1948 and for the next five years she sailed on the Australia run. In 1953 she became a one-class tourist ship and until 1960 she also cruised out of Australian ports for the Australian cruise market.

In December 1961 she was withdrawn and sold for scrapping in Spain where she arrived in March 1962.

ORPHEUS

Orpheus, on charter to Swan Hellenic, enters Lisbon. (Clive Harvey)

Swan Hellenic
5,092 GRT
Built in 1948 by Harland &
Wolff, Belfast
318 cruise passengers

Built as the *Munster* for the Irish Sea service of the British and Irish Steam Packet Co. as a post-war replacement for a ship of the same name that had been lost during the war.

As an Irish Sea ferry she could accommodate 1,500 passengers. In 1948 the demand for car transportation between Britain and Ireland was not foreseen although the ship had accommodation for up to 484 head of cattle!

By 1967 the ferry customers were demanding drive-on drive-off car ferries and the *Munster* and her sister *Leinster* were put up for sale. *Munster* was bought by the Company of Greece in 1968 and refitted as a cruise ship. She was to have been named *Theseus* but during the refit the name was changed to *Orpheus*.

She undertook Mediterranean, Alaskan and Caribbean cruises for her new owners until Swan Hellenic chartered her in 1974. Although she undertook some other charters, from then until 1995 she became a much-loved cultural haven for the 'Loyal Swans' as the company's repeat passengers are known. A merger of Greek cruise operators including Epirotiki led to the formation of Royal Olympic Cruises and *Orpheus* sailed under the new brand until she was laid up and scrapped in 2001.

ORSOVA

Orient Line/P&O

29,091 GRT

685 first, 800 tourist class passengers

The last ship to come out as a pure Orient Line vessel (the *Oriana* of 1960 was ordered by Orient Line but entered service after the merger with P&O), *Orsova* had a similar appearance to *Orcades* and *Oronsay*. She was fitted with air conditioning in 1960 and was in refit when the company merged with P&O although it would be 1965 before she was registered to the new concern. The ship operated summer cruises from Southampton for 685 first class and 800 second class passengers. She was never converted to one-class. Even in 1972 there were first class inside cabins with bunk beds and no toilet facilities!

Late in 1973 it was announced that *Canberra* was to be withdrawn and that *Orsova* and *Oriana* would operate the UK market cruises for P&O. *Canberra*'s draft was slightly greater than that of *Oriana* and it was believed that the latter would be able to enter more ports. The conversion of *Orsova* to a one-class ship was, however, deemed too costly and *Canberra* was reprieved, refitted as a one-class ship in 1974 with accommodation for 1,641 cruise passengers and gave over twenty years more service in the UK cruise market. *Orsova* was withdrawn in 1973 and scrapped on Taiwan in early 1974.

Originally *Orsova* was to replace *Canberra* but *Orsova* was scrapped and *Canberra* went on from strength to strength. (Clive Harvey)

OTRANTO (1909)

Orient Line

12,124 GRT

Built in 1909 by Workman Clark of Belfast

300 first class, 140 second class & 850 third class passengers

One of five similar ships built 1909 for the Australia service. Of the five sisters only *Otranto* made a significant number of cruises. Even before her maiden voyage to Australia *Otranto* made a series of cruises to the Norwegian fjords and the Baltic. Between 1910 and 1914 she was used during the summer months for cruises to both the Mediterranean and the Norwegian fjords.

In 1914 she was commissioned as HMS *Otranto*, an Armed Merchant Cruiser (AMC), and joined the squadron of Admiral Craddock in South America. The squadron consisted of the obsolete armoured cruisers HMS *Good Hope* and HMS *Monmouth*, the old battleship HMS *Canopus* and the modern light cruiser HMS *Glasgow*. Without the support of HMS *Canopus*, which was escorting colliers up from the Falkland Islands, the squadron met the German Asiatic Squadron of Admiral Von Spree off Coronel in Southern Chile on the late afternoon of 1 November 1914. Von Spree had two modern armoured cruisers, SMS *Scharnhorst* (flagship) and SMS *Gneisenau*, plus the light cruisers SMS *Nurnberg*, SMS *Leipzig* and SMS *Dresden*.

Out-gunned, Admiral Craddock, flying his flag in HMS *Good Hope*, initially ordered the vulnerable *Otranto* to remain with the squadron – probably to afford her protection. As the Germans started firing at her however, her captain quite rightly hauled off and made his escape into the gathering night. Within less than an hour both HMS *Good Hope* and HMS *Monmouth* had been sunk with all hands. Nothing that *Otranto* could have done would have altered the result of the battle, only that she and her crew would have been lost. No criticism of the captain was made and the Admiralty endorsed his actions. Slightly damaged, HMS *Glasgow* fell back to the support of HMS *Canopus*, who escorted her back to the Falklands.

Just over a month later the Royal Navy had its revenge when a British squadron under the command of Vice-Admiral Doveton Sturdee, and which included the battlecruisers HMS *Invincible* and *Inflexible*, surprised Von Spree off the Falkland Islands on 8 December 1914 and sank all his ships with the exception of SMS *Dresden*. Neither Von Spree, nor his sons Otto and Heinrich who served in the squadron, survived. Dresden was cornered and surrendered on 14 March 1915.

After her adventures around Cape Horn and South America *Otranto* continued her naval service but was converted to a troopship in 1918. On 25 September 1918 she left New York with twelve officers and 691 soldiers from the US Army (plus two YMCA representatives) in a convoy of twelve troopships. *Otranto* carried the convoy commodore.

On Sunday 6 October, just a month and a week away from the Armistice, the convoy was off the island of Islay in Scotland and the weather was foul with storm force 11 winds. The P&O steamer *Kashmir*, still operating as an AMC and forming the port escort to the convoy, made a turn to starboard whilst the *Otranto* turned to port. The ship's captains had both read the situation regarding the proximity of land differently – the later inquiry decided that they were equally to blame.

Kashmir collided with the port side of *Otranto*. With the ship in grave peril her consorts stood by to aid the evacuation. Whilst over 600 soldiers and crew were saved, nearly 400 were lost including the captain. There is a cemetery for those lost on the *Otranto* at Kilchoman on Islay and a monument erected by the American Red Cross on the southernmost tip of the island. *Kashmir* reached the Clyde with no casualties.

OTRANTO (1926)

Orient Line
20,026 GRT
Built in 1926 by Vickers,
Barrow-in-Furness
572 first & 1,114 second class
passengers

The third ship of a class of five, *Otranto* was preceded by her sisters *Orama* (1924) and *Oronsay* (1925). Like them she interspersed her mail runs to Australia with summer cruises to the Mediterranean and the Norwegian fjords. She survived her service as a troopship during the Second World War and was refitted for the carrying of emigrants from the UK to Australia during 1948. She stayed in this trade until 1957 when she was withdrawn and broken up at Feline in Scotland.

PACIFIC PRINCESS (1975)

19,907 GRT
Built in 1970 by Rheinstahl
Nordseewerke (Emden)
767 passengers

Together with her sister ship *Island Princess*, she was a ship that may have been responsible more than any other for introducing people to cruising. Owned by Flagship Cruises and originally named *Sea Venture*, she became *Pacific Princess* and was part of the small Princess Cruise fleet of Stanley B. McDonald acquired together with *Pacific Princess* and the Princess operation by P&O in 1974. Both ships became the stars of the highly popular *Love Boat*® television series and appeared on millions of television sets both in North America and the UK weekly. Both ships developed a very loyal following of not just North American but also UK customers.

In 2002 she was withdrawn and sold eventually becoming the *Pacific* of the Spanish cruise operator Pullmantur. Under the same name she is now owned by CVC, a Brazilian operator. She is scheduled to spend six months per year in Europe operating for Spanish operator Quail Cruises.

.

Opposite above: The final voyage of the original *Pacific Princess* in 2002. (Princess Cruises)

Opposite below: The swimming pool on the original *Pacific Princess*. (Roger Cartwright)

PACIFIC PRINCESS (2003)

30,277 GRT
Built in 199 by Chantiers de
l'Atlantique, France
688 passengers

Built as the *R Three* she was one of the identical 'R' ships built for Renaissance Cruises between 1998 and 2001. Renaissance Cruises suffered heavily after 11 September 2001 and with the company in dire financial straits all of the ships were placed on the market. In addition to *R Three*, P&O also acquired two more of these vessels; a sister ship for *Pacific Princess*, *Tahitian Princess* and *Minerva 2*.

PACIFIC SKY – see SKY PRINCESS

PACIFIC STAR

P&O Cruises (Australia)
36,674 GRT
Built in 1982 by Aalborg Vaerft
(Denmark)
1,022 passengers

The first new-build for Carnival Cruises she was named *Tropicale* and was a very distinctive vessel with the winged funnel that has become a trademark of Carnival Cruises. In 2001 she was transferred to Costa Cruises, Carnival having acquired Costa in 1997. Her distinctive funnel was replaced and she was renamed *Costa Tropicale*. Following the Carnival / P&O merger in 2003 the practice of transferring ships within the Carnival Group was expanded with Carnival's *Jubilee* becoming *Pacific Sun* in late 2004, being joined by *Costa Tropicale* as *Pacific Star* also in 2004, both ships being intended for the growing Australian cruise market – a traditional P&O area of operations. In 2008 she became the *Ocean Dream* of Pullmantur.

PACIFIC SUN

P&O Cruises (Australia)
47,262 GRT
Built in 1986 by Kockums
(Sweden)
1486 passengers

Built as *Jubilee*, an enlarged *Tropicale* for Carnival Cruises. Following the Carnival / P&O merger in 2003 the practice of transferring ships within the Carnival Group was expanded with Carnival's *Jubilee* becoming *Pacific Sun* in late 2004, being joined by *Costa Tropicale* as *Pacific Star* also in 2004, both ships being intended for the growing Australian cruise market – a traditional P&O area of operations.

RAJPUTANA

P&O

16,644 GRT

Built in 1925 by Harland &
Wolff, Greenock

310 first class & 290 second
class passengers

One of the four 'R' class ships built for P&O's London-Bombay service.
During the low season for travel to India the ships operated Mediterranean
cruises for UK cruise passengers in the years up to the Second World War.

Rajputana, like the other 'R' ships, was converted to an Armed Merchant
Cruiser (AMC) in 1939 and was sunk by *U108* on 13 April 1941.

RANCHI

P&O

16,738 GRT

Built in 1925 by Hawthorne
Leslie, Newcastle

310 first class & 290 second
class passengers

One of the four 'R' class ships built for P&O's London-Bombay service.
During the low season for travel to India the ships operated Mediterranean
cruises for UK cruise passengers in the years up to the Second World War.

Ranchi, like the other 'R' ships, was converted to an Armed Merchant
Cruiser (AMC) in 1939 and then to a repair ship for the Royal Navy in 1944.
Returned to P&O, in 1948 her accommodation was altered and she became
a one-class ship carrying up to 970 emigrants from the UK to Australia.
She was withdrawn from service in 1953 and scrapped at Newport, South
Wales.

RANPURNA

P&O

16,688 GRT

Built in 1924 by Hawthorne
Leslie, Newcastle

310 first class & 290 second
class passengers

One of the four 'R' class ships built for P&O's London-Bombay service.
During the low season for travel to India the ships operated Mediterranean
cruises for UK cruise passengers in the years up to the Second World War.

Ranpurna, like the other 'R' ships, was converted to an Armed Merchant
Cruiser (AMC) in 1939 and was purchased outright by the UK Government
in 1942 to become a fleet repair ship. She kept her name although adding
HMS and was broken up in Italy in 1961.

RAWALPINDI

P&O
16,644 GRT
Built in 1925 by Harland &
Wolff, Greenock
310 first class & 290 second
class passengers

One of the four 'R' class ships built for P&O's London-Bombay service. During the low season for travel to India the ships operated Mediterranean cruises for UK cruise passengers in the years up to the Second World War.

Rawalpindi, like the other 'R' ships, was converted to an Armed Merchant Cruiser (AMC) in 1939. On 23 November 1939 she was attacked and sunk by the German battlecruisers *Scharnhorst* and *Gneisenau* whilst patrolling off Iceland. Two hundred and seventy-five of her mainly reservist crew were lost, there being twenty-six survivors picked up by the German ships and another eleven by the *Chitral*, another P&O ship also serving as an AMC.

REGAL PRINCESS

Princess Cruises/P&O
(Australia)
70,285 GRT
Built in 1991 by Fincantieri
1,590 passengers

Regal Princess and her sister *Crown Princess* were ordered by Sitmar prior to the 1988 takeover by P&O. The largest P&O vessels up to that date, they present a striking appearance with the area over the bridge designed to resemble a dolphin.

Regal Princess remained with Princess when *Crown Princess* was transferred to the German market as *Aida Blu* and later *Rosa Blu*. In 2006 it was announced that she would be transferred to the P&O Australia operation to replace *Pacific Sky*, ex-*Sky Princess*. As *Pacific Dawn* she is the largest vessel yet dedicated to the Australia cruise market.

Royal Princess of 1984 in the Panama Canal. (Princess Cruises)

ROYAL PRINCESS (1984)

Princess Cruises/P&O Cruises
44,348 GRT
Built in 1984 by Wartsila
(Finland)
1,200 cruise passengers

This ship was the first since the *Wilhelm Gusloff* of the Nazi 'Strength through Joy' movement in the late 1930s to offer all outside accommodation. Of sleek, striking appearance she was revolutionary in that the vast majority of her accommodation was above the public rooms. Previously liners and cruise ships had been built with the public rooms above most of the passenger accommodation with only suites and other premium cabins being above the public rooms. Named by Diana Princess of Wales, her transfer to the UK market from 2005 with the name *Artemis* was announced in 2004. As *Artemis* she has taken on an 'adults only' cruising role.

Artemis is the Greek version of the Roman Goddess Diana (the goddess of hunting), a link with the lady who named the ship originally.

ROYAL PRINCESS (2007) – see MINERVA

RUBY PRINCESS

Princess Cruises
112,500 GRT
Built in 2008 by Fincantieri
3,599 passengers

Sister to *Emerald Princess* and *Crown Princess*. Due to debut November 2008.

SAPPHIRE PRINCESS

Princess Cruises
115,875 GRT
Built in 2004 by Mitsubishi
2,674 passengers

Very similar to *Caribbean Princess*, she was laid down as *Diamond Princess* as the lead ship of an enlarged *Grand Princess* type. Whilst under construction in Japan a fire broke out, delaying completion. In order to keep to schedule, *Sapphire Princess*, her sister also completing in the same yard, was renamed *Diamond Princess* with the original *Diamond Princess* becoming *Sapphire Princess*.

SEA PRINCESS (1978)

Princess Cruises/P&O Cruises
28,891 GRT
Built in 1966 by John Brown, Glasgow
778 passengers

Originally named *Kungsholm*, she was operated by Swedish-America on both transatlantic voyages and cruises. She was sold to Flagship Cruises in 1975 and operated out of New York. She was then acquired by the Princess Cruises operation of P&O in 1978 as *Sea Princess*. An extensive refit saw the removal of her forward funnel and the remodelling of the aft one, plus extensive alterations to her fittings – to the detriment of her appearance according to many purists.

In 1982 she was transferred to the UK P&O fleet as the running mate to *Canberra*. In 1995 she was given an 'ia' ending name to fit in with the naming of the ships of the UK P&O Cruises fleet. As *Victoria* she operated alongside *Oriana* and *Aurora* until her sale into the German cruise market in 2002 as the *Mona Lisa*. In this guise she can be recognised by the large portrait of the famous lady on her funnel. She is currently operating as the *Scholarship*. This is a recognised academic program aboard a transformed passenger ship hosting students on semester-long voyages around the world.

The spoiler of the *Grand Princess* class was dispensed with in later vessels. *Sapphire Princess* takes on passengers in Sydney. (Roger Cartwright)

After *Victoria* was sold to become the *Mona Lisa* she acquired an unusual funnel decoration. (Roger Cartwright)

In 1999 - 2000 *Victoria* was chartered by a resurrected Union-Castle Line to operate a round-Africa Millennium cruise and her funnel was painted in the Red and Black of Union-Castle although the hull remained white. For these voyages items of original Union Castle artwork were placed on board.

Victoria as *Mona Lisa* berthed at Grenada. (Roger Cartwright)

SEA PRINCESS (1998)

Princess Cruises - P&O Cruises – Princess Cruises
77,499 GRT
Built in 1998 by Fincantieri, Italy
2,016 cruise passengers

With the disposal of *Victoria* and the re-branding of *Acadia* as *Ocean Village*, the *Sea Princess* was transferred from the US to the UK P&O Princess operation in May 2003 and renamed *Adonia*. *Adonia* together with the slightly newer *Oceana* (ex-*Ocean Princess*) formed the two new 'White Sisters', reintroducing a term used for the *Strathaird* and the *Strathnaver* in the early 1930s.

Refitted to appeal to UK rather than US cruise passengers, the *Adonia* and her sister feature the latest in cruise ship interior design with large atriums together with glass-walled lifts.

With the rebranding of *Acadia* as *Ocean Village*, *Adonia* took on the role of adults-only ship and undertook a world cruise in 2004. In April 2004 however it was announced that the ship would be transferred back to the Princess operation under her original name in May 2005 when the new *Arcadia* joined the fleet. As *Sea Princess* she operates cruises under the Princess brand but designed specifically for UK-based passengers, a role to be taken over by *Grand Princess* in 2009.

SKY PRINCESS

Princess Cruises – P&O Cruises (Australia)
46,087 GRT
Built in 1984 by CNM La Seyne (France)
1,200 passengers

Laid down as the *Fairsky* for Sitmar she became a Princess vessel with the takeover of Sitmar by P&O in 1988. She was renamed *Sky Princess*. Notable as being one of the last passenger vessels to use steam turbines (this left her remarkably free of vibrations), she was a regular Princess operator in the Far East. It was not surprising therefore that she was transferred to the Australian operation in 2000 to replace the *Fair Princess*. Renamed *Pacific Sky*, her age and her complicated machinery led to problems, with cruises having to be cancelled. In May 2006 she left the P&O fleet having been purchased by the Spanish cruise operator Pullmantur as *Sky Wonder*.

SPIRIT OF LONDON

P&O Cruises/Princess Cruises
17,370 GRT
Built by Cantieri Navali del Tirreno e Riuniti
700 cruise passengers

Spirit of London was P&O's first purpose-built cruise ship. A small vessel, she was purchased from her original Norwegian owners whilst building. P&O introduced her to the US market for West Coast cruises in November 1971. Following the acquisition of Princess Cruises she was transferred to the new company as the *Sun Princess*. In 1988 she was sold to Premier Cruise Lines as the *Majestic*, later renamed *Starship Majestic*. In 1997 she became the *Flamenco* of Festival Cruises and when that company failed in 2004 she was laid up before becoming the *New Flamenco* of Travelplan Cruises, a Spanish operator.

In 2001 P&O very nearly acquired Festival Cruises and had this happened the ship would have re-entered the P&O fleet.

STAR PRINCESS

Princess Cruises – P&O Cruises – Ocean Village
63,524 GRT
Built in 1989 by Chantiers de L'Atlantique, France
1,624 passengers

Ordered as the *Sitmar Fairmajesty* but launched as *Star Princess*. Princess Cruises (owned by P&O) had acquired Sitmar in 1988 just after the ship was laid down. The ship has a striking profile that was quite revolutionary at the time. She was transferred from Princess Cruises to P&O Cruises in the UK in December 1997 as the replacement for the *Canberra* and renamed *Arcadia*. In her first season the ship carried a superb collection of US contemporary art but this was removed and works of art from the UK were substituted. The majority of standard cabins on *Arcadia* were somewhat larger than the norm and this gained her the nickname of 'the spaceship'!

Star Princess was eventually acquired by Carnival's great rival Royal Caribbean to operate as *Sky Wonder* for their Spanish operation, Pullmatur. (Roger Cartwright)

Arcadia, ex-*Star Princess*, was nicknamed 'spaceship' due to her extra spacious cabins.

In 2002 *Arcadia* was designated as an 'adults only' ship, a role that was taken on by *Adonia* when *Arcadia* was renamed *Ocean Village* in 2003.

In 2003 P&O / Princess Cruises, as the company was renamed in 2000 following the demerger of the cruise interests from the P&O parent company, announced a new venture – Ocean Village. Designed for the 'thirty something, dress-down Friday set', *Ocean Village*, as *Arcadia* was renamed, offers a resort cruise experience with a very relaxed ambience. Meals are buffet style and there are plenty of dining options. Shore activities include a number of sporting opportunities – cruise passengers can even rent a mountain bike direct from the ship. Port stays are longer than the traditional norm of arriving early morning and leaving just before dinner. The ship will relocate to the P&O Australia operation in 2010.

STAR PRINCESS

Princess Cruises
108,997 GRT
Built in 2002 by Fincanteri
3,102 max. passengers

The third of the *Grand Princess* class, she retains the 'spoiler' at the stern, a feature that has been dispensed with in later vessels.

Star Princess enters Juneau, Alaska. (Roger Cartwright)

STRATHALLAN

P&O
23,722 GRT
Built in 1938 by Vickers
Armstrong, Barrow-in-Furness
448 first & 563 tourist class
passengers

The single-funnelled *Strathallan* is believed to have undertaken a number of cruises before her career was cut short off Oran supporting 'Operation Torch', an operation that also saw the loss of the *Viceroy of India*. *Strathallan* was torpedoed and sunk by *U562* on 21 December 1942.

STRATHAIRD

P&O
22,270 GRT
Built in 1932 by Vickers
Armstrong, Barrow-in-Furness
498 first & 668 tourist class
passengers

The second of the 'Strath' ships and sister to *Strathnaver*, she was the second of the 'White Sisters'. The two ships gained a loyal cruise following in the 1930s, offering a series of UK-based cruises in addition to their regular UK-Australia liner service.

Like *Strathnaver* she had her dummy first and second funnels removed after the war, being rebuilt with just a single funnel.

From 1954 onwards *Strathaird* operated a tourist class only service from the UK to Australia. She was broken up in 1961 at Hong Kong.

STRATHEDEN

P&O
23,732 GRT
Built in 1937 by Vickers
Armstrong, Barrow-in-Furness
448 first & 563 tourist class
passengers, later 1,200 tourist
class only

Sister to the short-lived *Strathallan* and half-sister to *Strathmore*, the single-funnelled *Stratheden* undertook a number of pre-war cruises. After the war she resumed her liner service, being sold in 1964 to become the *Henrietta Latsis*, being renamed *Marianna Latsis* in 1966. She was broken up in Italy in 1969. Just prior to her withdrawal from P&O service she was chartered in 1963 and 1964 together with *Strathmore* to the Travel Saving's Association, by which time she carried 1,200 passengers in tourist class.

STRATHMORE

P&O
23,428 GRT
Built in 1935 by Vickers
Armstrong, Barrow-in-Furness
445 first & 665 tourist class
passengers, later 1,200 tourist
class only

Half-sister to *Strathallan* and *Stratheden*, *Strathmore* reverted to steam turbines (as did her two half-sisters). She also had only one funnel instead of the three funnels of the two preceding 'Strath' ships.

She undertook a number of pre-war cruises and after the war she resumed her liner service, being sold in 1963 to become the *Marianna Latsi*, being renamed *Henrietta Latsi* in 1966. Just prior to her withdrawal from P&O service she was chartered in 1963 and 1964 together with *Stratheden* to the Travel Saving's Association, by which time she carried 1,200 passengers in tourist class. She was broken up in Italy in 1969.

STRATHNAVER

22,547 GRT
Built in 1931 by Vickers
Armstrong, Barrow-in-Furness
500 first class & 670 tourist
class passengers

The first of the 'White Sisters', she was a sister ship to the *Strathaird*. These vessels introduced the white hull and yellow funnel to the P&O fleet, previous vessels having carried a livery of black hull and black funnels. The term 'White Sisters' was re-introduced in 2003 for the *Adonia* and *Oceana*.

The two ships gained a loyal cruise following in the 1930s, offering a series of UK-based cruises in addition to their regular UK-Australia liner service.

Strathnaver had her dummy first and second funnels removed after the war, being rebuilt with just a single funnel.

From 1954 onwards *Strathnaver* operated a tourist class only service from the UK to Australia. She was broken up in 1962 at Hong Kong.

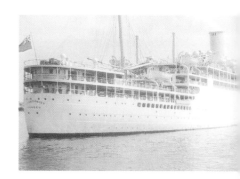

Even reduced to one funnel, *Strathnaver* presents a classic profile. (Clive Harvey)

SUN PRINCESS (1978) – see SPIRIT OF LONDON

TAHITIAN PRINCESS

30,277 GRT
Built in 1999 by Chantiers de l'Atlantique, France
688 passengers

Built as the *R Four* she was one of the identical 'R' ships built for Renaissance Cruises between 1998 and 2001. Renaissance Cruises suffered heavily after 11 September 2001 and with the company in dire financial straits all of the ships were placed on the market. In addition to *R Four*, P&O also acquired two more of these vessels; a sister ship for *Tahitian Princess*, *Pacific Princess*, and *Minerva 2*. *Tahitian Princess* will be renamed in 2009, becoming *Ocean Princess*. The new name is intended to reflect the ship's new deployment on worldwide itineraries. The renaming will take place while the ship is out of service during a routine maintenance period in Singapore in November 2009. *Pacific Princess* will then provide cruises from Papeete, Tahiti, where the *Tahitian Princess* has been based.

UGANDA

British India
16,907 GRT
Built in 1952 by Barclay Curle & Co. Ltd, Glasgow
306 cabin passengers and 920 pupils

Uganda was built for British India's London to East Africa service, and spent fifteen years on the route with her sister, *Kenya*. Increased competition from the airlines as well as the changes to the pattern of trading following the gaining of independence by the countries she was built to serve, as well as the closure of the Suez Canal in 1967, brought about the demise of British India's East Africa route. Before her withdrawal from service the company had already announced that she would be rebuilt as a schools ship.

The work was undertaken in Germany and took from March 1967 to February 1968. It was an extensive rebuild, incorporating classrooms and dormitories in what had formerly been cargo spaces, and creating two lido areas: one forward for the 306 cabin passengers and one aft for the 920 children. The original first class public rooms remained relatively unchanged, for the use of the cabin passengers, but many of the cabins were also rebuilt.

She sailed from Southampton on 27 February 1968 on her first cruise, to the Mediterranean. Her normal pattern of employment was on cruises from various British ports during the summer months to Scandinavia and the Baltic and to the Atlantic Islands. In the late summer she would then reposition to the Mediterranean and operate fly cruises throughout the winter.

Uganda occasionally operated cruises under charter to various organis-ations such as the National Trust of Scotland. *Uganda* became probably the most popular of the schools ships and built up a very loyal following among her cabin passengers, many of whom returned year after year. In December 1972 British India ceased to exist as a separate entity and both *Uganda* and *Nevasa* were transferred to the ownership of P&O. From 1973 they were marketed under the BI Discovery Cruises banner, retaining the British India funnel colours.

In April 1982 she was requisitioned by the Government to become a hospital ship during the Falklands conflict. She returned to Southampton four months later, in August, and was given a refit converting her back into a cruise ship. This, however, was only a brief return to commercial service (thus bringing to an end the British India school ship concept) as she was chartered in January 1983 by the Ministry of Defence to provide troop transport between the Falkland Islands and Ascension Island. The charter was for two years, after which she was laid up in the River Fal and was later sold to be broken up in Taiwan. While at anchor near Kaohsiung she was driven ashore by a typhoon and capsized onto her side and was gradually broken up in situ.

VECTIS

P&O
5,627 GRT
Built in 1881 by Caird & Co., Glasgow
150 passengers

Built for the UK-Australian mail service of P&O, the ship was originally named the *Rome* and was converted for cruising in 1904 and renamed *Vectis*. As the *Rome* she had accommodation for 187 first and forty-six second class passengers but for cruising she carried only 160, making her extremely spacious in her cruising guise. She marked P&O's entry into the cruise market and was sold to the French Government in 1912 but saw little service under the French flag as she was sold for scrapping to an Italian company in 1913.

VENTURA

P&O Cruises
115,000 GRT
Ordered from Fincantieri (Italy)
in 2005
3,100 cruise passengers

Similar to *Caribbean Princess* but with an internal layout suited to the UK cruise market, the ship made her debut in 2008. Easily the largest vessel ever constructed for the UK market she was named at Southampton in some style by the actress Dame Helen Mirren. With a large number of entertainment venues, ten alternative dining options and dedicated facilities for children of all ages, she is the UK market's first mega ship and a fine addition to the fleet. Her interior designs by Nick Munro and her artwork are designed for UK customers and she represents a fine investment in the UK market. A sister is planned for 2010.

VICEROY OF INDIA

19,648 GRT
Built in 1928 by Alexander
Stephen, Glasgow
415 first & 258 second class
passengers

Designed for the UK-India service, *Viceroy of India* (the original intention had been to name her *Taj Mahal*) was only the third vessel in the world to be fitted with turbo-electric machinery, the use of which made her a fast ship compared with others in the fleet. *Viceroy of India* brought a new standard of luxury to the UK-India service.

Beautifully appointed, she made regular cruises from Southampton throughout the 1930s, venturing as far as the Caribbean and the South Atlantic.

Acting as a troopship for the 'Operation Torch' landings in North Africa in November 1942, *Viceroy of India* was returning from the landings empty of troops when she was torpedoed and sunk off Oran by *U407* on 11 November 1942 with the loss of four lives.

VICTORIA – see SEA PRINCESS (1978)

Ventura sets sail after her naming in 2008. She is the largest cruise liner ever built for the UK market. (Mike O'Dwyer)

Bibliography

Aurora – Dawn of a New Era. (P&O)

Canberra – In the Wake of a Legend, Lord Sterling, Geoffrey Dawson & Captain Rory Smith. (Conway Maritime Press)

Cruise –Identity, Design and Culture, Peter Quartermaine and Bruce Peter. (Laurence King)

Cruise Britannia (second edition), Roger Cartwright & Clive Harvey. (The History Press)

Cruise Ships (second edition), William Mayes. (Overview Press)

Cruise Ships – An Evolution in Design, Philip Dawson. (Conway)

Devils on the Deep Blue Sea, Kristopher A. Garin. (Plume)

Glory Days – P&O, David L. Williams. (Ian Allan)

Liners to the Sun, John Maxton-Graham. (Sheridan House)

Merchant Fleets – British India S N Co, Duncan Haws. (Shield Publications)

Merchant Fleets: P&O Lines, Norman L. Middlemiss. (Shield Publications)

Passenger Ships of the Orient Line, Neil McCart. (PSL)

Selling the Sea, Bob Dickinson & Andy Vladimir. (Wiley)

SS Canberra, William H. Miller. (Tempus)

The Ballad of Oriana. (P&O)

The British Merchant Navy – Images and Impressions, Paintings by Robert Lloyd, Robert Lloyd. (Ships in Focus)

The Cruise Ship – A Very British Institution, Nick Robins. (The History Press)

The Development and Growth of the Cruise Industry, Roger Cartwright & Carolyn Baird. (Butterworth Heinemann)

The Sitmar Line & the V Ships, Maurizio Eliseo. (Carmania Press)

The Story of P&O, David & Stephen Howarth. (Weidenfeld & Nicolson)

Visit our website and discover thousands of other History Press books.
www.thehistorypress.co.uk